A DESCENDING SPIRAL

A DESCENDING SPIRAL

Exposing the Death Penalty in 12 Essays

Marc Bookman

THE
NEW
PRESS

NEW YORK
LONDON

The following essays were previously published in slightly different form:

"Executed Against the Judgment of Twelve Jurors" was originally published in
The Atlantic. "How Crazy Is Too Crazy to Be Executed?" was originally published
in *Mother Jones*. "Sex-Shamed to Death" was originally published in *The Appeal*.
"The Lawyer Who Drank His Client to Death" was originally published in
Mother Jones. "When a Kid Kills His Longtime Abuser, Who's the Victim?"
was originally published in *Mother Jones*. "The Confessions of Innocent Men"
was originally published in *The Atlantic*. "A Descending Spiral" was originally
published in *Mother Jones*. "Trials and Errors" was originally published in *Slate*.
"The N-Word in the Jury Box" was originally published in *Mother Jones*. "Smoke"
was originally published in *University Of Missouri–Kansas City Law Review*.

Requests for permission to reproduce selections from this book should
be made through our website: https://thenewpress.com/contact.

Published in the United States by The New Press, New York, 2021
Distributed by Two Rivers Distribution

ISBN 978-1-62097-654-8 (hc)
ISBN 978-1-62097-659-3 (ebook)
CIP data is available

The New Press publishes books that promote and enrich public discussion and
understanding of the issues vital to our democracy and to a more equitable world.
These books are made possible by the enthusiasm of our readers; the support
of a committed group of donors, large and small; the collaboration of our many
partners in the independent media and the not-for-profit sector; booksellers, who
often hand-sell New Press books; librarians; and above all by our authors.

www.thenewpress.com

Composition by dix!
This book was set in Fairfield LH

Printed in the United States of America

2   4   6   8   10   9   7   5   3   1

*For Aubs, Jossie, and Kyle, and the dumb
luck that brought them to me*

The ultimate weakness of violence is that it is a descending spiral, begetting the very thing it seeks to destroy.

—Martin Luther King Jr.

Contents

A DESCENDING SPIRAL

1

Executed Against the
Judgment of Twelve Jurors

The capricious nature of the death penalty was on full display on August 5, 2013, when the state of Florida executed John Errol Ferguson. More than three decades had come and gone since he'd received a death sentence for his role in what came to be known as the Carol City killings. It was the longest time lapse between death sentence and execution in U.S. history, due largely to the extraordinary degree of mental illness Ferguson had exhibited since well before his arrest for the murders.

But in the hundreds of news stories about the Ferguson case, there was barely a word about Beauford White, one of the other men who had been with Ferguson during the murders. Perhaps it was because White had been executed twenty-six years earlier, and his name had faded from memory. Or perhaps the public had forgotten, or never known, that the jury convicting Beauford White didn't want him to be executed.

Jury verdicts are considered sacrosanct in American jurisprudence, particularly where the death penalty is concerned. Proponents of capital punishment have long argued that death sentences imposed by twelve jurors must be respected above any claims of bad lawyering, prosecutorial misconduct, judicial mistakes, or myriad other errors. Verdicts in capital cases are different than in all other cases in one crucial regard: the decision whether someone should live or die is a moral one, rather than factual or legal. Unlike a guilty verdict, which is reached through group deliberation, a life or death sentencing decision in a capital case is the product of individual reflection: each juror weighs the arguments for life imprisonment or execution on his or her own.

A majority of states that have capital punishment require a unanimous vote by a jury before the death penalty is imposed, but many people are on death row even though one or more jurors voted for life, and close to one hundred inmates are on death rows across eight states specifically because of a judge's decision to vote for death. In recent years the two states that still allowed judges to override a majority of jurors—Florida and Alabama—have passed laws prohibiting the practice. Those laws were not retroactive, however, and close to three dozen people remain eligible for execution after the majority of jurors voted for life. This is how Beauford White came to be executed by a judge's decision to go against the wishes of his entire jury.

As a literary device, it might work well to trace the parallel lives of John Ferguson and Beauford White. But the truth is that their lives ran at opposing angles, at least as far as the crime and its aftermath were concerned. So the night of the Carol City killings is as good a place as any to start their story. On July 27, 1977, Ferguson, identifying himself as "Lucky" and posing as an employee of Florida Power and Light, entered a house in a suburb of Miami. Shortly thereafter, he pulled a gun and demanded drugs, money, and jewelry from the female inhabitant. His co-conspirators, Beauford White and a man named Marvin Francois, joined Ferguson inside the house; all of the men were armed. Eventually, seven more people entered the home, including the woman's boyfriend and the owner of the house.

At this point, the prosecution and defense versions of the story veer away from each other. The state claimed that the killers wanted to eliminate the witnesses; lawyers for White argued that their client was along for the robbery, but the murders were part of a prearranged contract involving only Ferguson and Francois. In either case, two facts were undisputed: Eight people had been forced to lie on the floor, their hands tied behind their backs, and shot in the back of the head (two miraculously survived). And Ferguson and Francois had pulled the triggers. This was not a whodunit.

Everyone agreed that White had never attempted to kill anyone, or even intended that anyone should be killed—that he had, in fact, tried to talk Ferguson and Francois out of killing. While White took his share of the drugs, money, and jewelry, the testimony revealed that he appeared to be in shock after the murders, his eyes glazed over and his expression blank, "just sitting there like he seen a ghost," according to a co-defendant who became the star witness for the state. And then there was this testimony of his refusal to cover up the crime, from the man who drove the killers to the crime scene:

> Q: Somebody said something about getting rid of the .38, I think is what you said before we took the break.
> A: Yes. Marvin [Francois] and Ferguson was talking about getting rid of the guns. They asked Beauford to get rid of it.
> Q: What did Beauford say?
> A: Beauford said, "I ain't getting rid of nothing."

So the picture was clearly drawn for the jury: Beauford White had not killed or attempted to kill—had, in fact, been shocked that killing had occurred—and was unwilling to join in the cover-up afterward. When the jury sat down to decide if White was the worst of the worst, it wasn't even close. All twelve voted that life imprisonment for him was more appropriate than execution.

John Ferguson did not fare nearly as well in front of his jury. Logic dictated that he was the leader—at the very least, he was the first to enter the house and pull a gun, the first to bind and blindfold a victim—and it was clear that Ferguson, along with Francois, had placed the eight victims on the floor and shot them in the back of their heads. While there was evidence that Ferguson had been mentally ill for some years before the date of the crime, he was clearly sane under any legal definition of insanity, and with six murders and two near misses on the docket, the jurors were deliberating one of the worst crimes in the history of southern Florida. At the end of May 1978, less than a year after the slaughter in Carol City, the jury unanimously recommended that John Errol Ferguson be executed by the state.

It is reasonable to wonder how Beauford White, the man who received a unanimous jury vote for life, came to be executed in 1987, while John Ferguson managed to avoid a similar fate until 2013, even with a unanimous vote for death. There is no single explanation, as there rarely is when the death penalty is concerned, but a good starting point is the Florida sentencing law at that time.

When every state capital punishment law was ruled unconstitutional in the landmark 1972 case *Furman v. Georgia*, Florida became the first state to pass a new death penalty statute, six months later. Most of the country soon followed suit, but Florida's law had a quirk that only Alabama and Delaware adopted: The jury's vote regarding life or death was a *recommendation*, not a decision. The trial judge alone would determine the sentence.

Two years later, however, the Florida Supreme Court weighted the jury recommendation: For a judge to override a jury vote and change a life vote to a death verdict, "the facts suggesting a sentence of death should be so clear and convincing that virtually no reasonable person could differ." Regardless of what the jurors thought, the facts, and Beauford White's fate, rested with the trial judge, Richard S. Fuller.

Judge Fuller was a scoutmaster, a medic in a MASH unit, and a personal injury lawyer. Tall, distinguished, and with a memorable head of white hair, he is recalled by South Florida lawyers as the guy you might select if you were looking to cast a judge in a movie. One of those same lawyers remembered him in a legal brief as a man "who would send an individual to the electric chair." He presided over the consecutive jury trials of the three defendants in the Carol City killings, and Beauford White found himself sandwiched between the two actual killers.

Marvin Francois was first, and when the jury recommended a death sentence, Judge Fuller followed their recommendation three days before the Beauford White trial started. When imposing a sentence in a capital case, a Florida judge is obligated to determine reasons a defendant should live and reasons he should die—these are called mitigating and aggravating circumstances—and then weigh them to determine the sentence. Judge Fuller found no mitigating circumstances in Francois's case. (His future appeals proved fruitless, and he was executed in 1985.)

Beauford White's case was surely much more complicated than Francois's. The crime itself was horrific, but White had not taken part in the killings, and had in fact argued against them. Twelve jurors heard the evidence and voted to spare him, no small fact according to the Florida Supreme Court. Were their voices to be ignored? Could anyone have said that no *reasonable* person would have voted for life, after twelve citizens selected randomly from the community just had?

Yes—Judge Richard S. Fuller. In weighing the arguments for a death sentence against those for a life sentence, Judge Fuller once again found no mitigating circumstances—not White's failure to kill, not his shock after the killings, not even his opposition to the killings. At the end of April 1978, Beauford White was sentenced to death.

In May, John Ferguson's jury unanimously recommended death, and Judge Fuller imposed that sentence as well. Of the three decisions, this one was likely the easiest for the judge: only a month before, Ferguson had confessed to killing two seventeen-year-olds in the course of a robbery/rape, a crime that six months later resulted in two more death sentences imposed by the same judge. There was some evidence that Ferguson had mental health problems—he had been committed previously to a state mental hospital—but Judge Fuller was not sufficiently moved to consider his mental illness a mitigating circumstance. In fact, as with Francois and White, Judge Fuller found no mitigating circumstances at all for John Ferguson.

The cases moved on to the Florida Supreme Court. The Ferguson litigation hit a little speed bump when the court found that Judge Fuller had misapplied the law regarding mental illness as a mitigating circumstance. But another judge ran through the procedure properly and reimposed a death sentence.

Beauford White's sentence didn't meet with any resistance at all—the court had no problem affirming Fuller's decision to override a unanimous jury, ruling that "the only colorable mitigating circumstance was the . . . consideration that the defendant was not the triggerman."

Colorable? That was a strange way to put it, particularly since all twelve jurors had found White's lack of participation in the murders as the reason to recommend a life sentence. Indeed, the foreman of the jury, in an interview almost ten years after White's trial, said, "We voted for life because we did not see a shred of evidence indicating that White himself actually took part in the killing. We knew he was present, and we knew he was guilty of something, we just didn't know of what crime it was. We couldn't be sure he was guilty of murder, so we voted to spare his life."

But it didn't matter what the foreman thought—or what anyone else on the jury thought, for that matter. Judge Fuller had decided that the jury was wrong, and the Florida Supreme Court had found his decision "so clear and convincing that virtually no reasonable person could differ."

Capital cases follow a well-worn appellate path, and the next stop for White and Ferguson was post-conviction. This is the stage where defendants go back to the trial court and allege mistakes or omissions that took place the first time around. But while both men found themselves at the same stage, their legal postures were profoundly different. Ferguson now had two more death sentences to deal with—the murders of the two seventeen-year-olds had been merged with the Carol City killings for purposes of his appeal—but his extensive mental health history and brutal upbringing had required a complex investigation that slowed his appeals dramatically.

White, on the other hand, had already persuaded every member of his jury that he should live. His post-conviction case took a very different turn from Ferguson's, and a considerably luckier one in two ways. His case was now in the hands of Judge Herbert Klein, a man far more predisposed toward mercy than Judge Fuller. And while White's case was pending, the U.S. Supreme Court had decided the Florida death penalty case of Earl Enmund.

Like Beauford White, Earl Enmund hadn't killed or attempted to kill anyone. And like White, Enmund was clearly guilty of a robbery during which people had been killed. Overruling the Florida Supreme Court, the U.S. Supreme Court determined that death was not a valid penalty for a person who neither took life, attempted to take life, nor intended to take life.

Enmund v. Florida appeared to be a home run for Beauford White. At least Judge Klein thought so; applying the *Enmund* case, he vacated White's death sentences, and the case once again went to the Florida Supreme Court.

Courts don't like to be reversed, and it is impossible to read the Florida court's opinion without feeling the justices' resentment: "We have no doubt that *Enmund*, overturning as it did centuries of law, represents a major change in constitutional law and that we are obligated to revisit this case in order to determine if *Enmund* prohibits the imposition of the death penalty under the facts and circumstances of this case."

Not surprisingly, the court found no prohibition. Stating that White had done nothing to "disassociate himself" from the murders, the Florida Supreme Court reimposed the death penalty on him. Not all seven justices agreed—two of them thought that the *Enmund* case required a life sentence for White, and one came right out and said that an appellate court had no business sentencing anyone to death, which was what it was doing by overruling Judge Klein.

But two negative votes did not change the outcome for Beauford White. On a Florida jury, even a unanimous recommendation was not the final word about life or death. But a simple majority was more than enough for the Florida Supreme Court.

Since Beauford White had received a life recommendation from all twelve of his jurors, his lawyers initially had little reason to contest the facts of the Carol City killings. But as the first President Adams said more than two hundred years ago while defending reviled British troops in the Boston Massacre case, facts are stubborn things. And as White's case wound its way through the courts on a profoundly dangerous spiral, some stubborn facts surrounding the crime itself began to surface. Not small facts, either—facts that raised questions about who the victims were, and how the investigation of the crime had been conducted.

The Florida Supreme Court had noted that "the essential facts" of the case were not in dispute: an hour after the robbery had begun, the owner of the house and five of his friends had "arrived," subsequently becoming victims of the robbery. One of those friends, Johnnie Hall, had survived the shooting and become the main witness for the state. But Hall was not the innocent bystander portrayed at the trial. And the lead investigator in the case, Detective Robert Derringer, was not the police officer the jury and judge might have assumed he was.

To understand who they really were, it is necessary to revisit the Miami of the late 1970s and early 1980s—a city drowning in cocaine and cash.

South Florida brought three things together in the late 1970s: proximity to Colombia, a landscape that lent itself to easy access by small planes and boats, and an extraordinary willingness by all branches of the government to look the other way. When the drug boom hit, fishermen stopped fishing and used their boats for drug imports. Luxury cars flew off lots, and the Miami Federal Reserve branch found itself with a surplus of $5 billion in $50 and $100 bills—more than the next twelve Federal Reserve branches in the country combined. And one other thing happened: Miami became the homicide capital of the country.

Law enforcement was not oblivious to Dade County's sudden shift in fortunes. While the Carol City victims initially seemed to have had the bad luck of walking in on a robbery, the police knew better. A police document written four days after the crime, but never revealed to the defense, summarized the true nature of the circumstances: "Charles Ceasar Stinson, 35, of Milwaukee, Wisconsin, was in Miami with the intention of making a large cocaine buy. Charles Stinson contacted his associate, Gilbert Williams, 35, of Miami, who is his contact in Miami, in an effort to arrange the cocaine deal. Gilbert Williams utilized John Hall, 45, to make the arrangements to buy the cocaine."

The memo went on to describe how the victims and the owner of the house had been involved in the drug deal. The fact that John Hall was an active player in a drug conspiracy, rather than an innocent man who happened to stumble into the wrong house, was only half the issue. At trial, Hall was the main witness in the case, and it was he who testified that the murders took place to eliminate the witnesses, rather than as a prearranged hit Beauford White had nothing to do with.

The cocaine, the violence, the incredible amounts of cash—all of these things had a predictable impact on the Dade County police force. A federal investigation in the early 1980s had revealed that during the period of the Carol City killings, the lead detective in the case, Robert Derringer, and another detective involved in the investigation, Fabio Alonso, had been deeply entangled with drug dealers and their profits.

In all, seven officers participating in the Carol City investigation were implicated in a large-scale drug operation that involved, among other things, stealing drugs, money, and jewelry from the residences of homicide victims. Derringer was ultimately convicted of income tax evasion and unlawful appropriation of property and sentenced to six years in federal prison. Alonso received a ten-year sentence.

Finally, there were considerable new revelations about Beauford White himself. His trial attorney had spent very little time looking into his own client's background—the law that requires such information to be taken into account in capital cases was in its infancy in the late 1970s when White's case first came to court. But nine years later, the obligation to discover, understand, and present a defendant's history was better known, and it turned out White's background was stark and sympathetic. His mother, who started having children at twelve and had had her fifth by the age of twenty, was routinely and savagely beaten by his father, Ernest—and when his father was not beating her, Beauford himself became the target. When he was three, his father knocked him out cold, driving his teeth through his tongue; a doctor later concluded that this assault and others were the likely cause of seizures that plagued Beauford through his lifetime.

When Ernest White left the family to go to Detroit, his mother took up with a series of men just as abusive, eventually killing one of them and going to prison for a seven-year sentence. Beauford, abandoned time and time again as a youngster and now without a mother or a father, nonetheless shone in school. Twenty-five years later, in a statement given to Beauford's lawyers, his junior high school principal recalled him as "an ideal young person . . . academically gifted . . . He probably would have been a straight-A student if he would have had some stability in the home and a place to study . . . one of those kids that a teacher looks forward to being around." Another teacher described him as "truly one of my tops"; a third said the reason she remembered him all those years later was because "I liked him so much."

He was reportedly a terrific athlete as well—Leroy Cromartie, a supervisor for the Miami Recreation Department, told the lawyers that Beauford had had "major league potential." (And Cromartie would have known—his son Warren was a successful first baseman and outfielder with the Montreal Expos.) Cromartie went on to detail the drug culture that eventually sucked Beauford into its maw, and the addiction that in the end overcame his potential. Then he said the same thing dozens of other witnesses had said: "It tears me up to see what happened to Beauford, but I know too well how it happened. I would have appreciated the chance to explain all of this to his judge and jury."

Was there time for these new revelations to save Beauford White? By now, his case had already been denied once in the federal courts, and his new lawyers—death penalty specialists who worked well under the pressure of an execution warrant—rushed to get the previously hidden information in front of a judge before it was too late.

With less than two weeks to go before White's scheduled execution, the Florida Supreme Court refused to even consider the new claims. "It is clear . . . that this eleventh hour petition is an abuse of process," the court wrote in an opinion that ran less than five hundred words. A request for a stay of execution a few days later compelled the same court to complain, "The fact that we are dealing with a death sentence does not excuse [White's lawyers'] failure to abide by the Florida Rules of Criminal Procedure." Time was running out.

*   *   *

While White was already in the homestretch of his last appeals, Ferguson's lawyers were still in state court, working to piece together their client's complex and dysfunctional background. There was no doubt that Ferguson had suffered from a serious mental illness since well before the crimes that had put him on death row, but the cause of the illness was proving impossible to pinpoint. As a child he had been forced to move nearly a dozen times, fleeing his violent and drunken father or his mother's many boyfriends; sometimes the family moved simply to find a place with electricity and running water. When he was thirteen, his father died from the effects of alcohol abuse, and shortly thereafter he was committed to a state school. He dropped out in ninth grade; a medical report indicated that he was "beat up by kids and . . . a loner throughout his life."

It hardly seems possible, but Ferguson's life took a severe turn for the worse when he was twenty-one: he was shot four times by the police, once in the head. Those around him noticed an immediate impact on his behavior, which often became irrational and inexplicably hostile. From the day he was shot to the day of his arrest in the Carol City killings, he spent the majority of his time in mental hospitals and the rest of it committing crimes; twice, he was found not guilty of robberies by reason of insanity. It was during this eight-year period from 1969 to 1977 that the true scope of John Ferguson's mental instability became known.

Psychiatry is not an exact science. Different doctors bring different perspectives to their examinations, and mental illnesses wax and wane. Thus, the consistency of Ferguson's diagnoses, through eleven evaluations by seven different doctors, is the most compelling evidence of just how ill he was. Virtually every evaluation echoed the same three words: schizophrenia, psychosis, and hallucinations. His symptoms were consistent as well—he was conversing with his deceased father, he refused to sleep in jail because "they" put scorpions on his bed, he suffered from headaches caused by roaches and "very small" people that had been placed inside his brain.

And every evaluation came with a warning or a recommendation: Ferguson had "such a severely damaged ability to distinguish between right and wrong" that he "would commit illegal acts," wrote one doctor. Warned another, his "degree of irrationality coupled with a rather impulsive, explosive and aggressive nature makes him a rather dangerous person both to himself and to others." A third concluded that he was "dangerous to the point where he is considered homicidal." Finally there was this: Ferguson "has a longstanding, severe illness which will most likely require long-term inpatient hospitalization. This man is dangerous and cannot be released under any circumstances."

More than forty years later, it's unclear what circumstances allowed a state mental hospital to release a paranoid schizophrenic despite his imminent danger to the public. But Ferguson was on the streets on July 27, 1977, when he participated in the Carol City killings. He would not be free much longer, and the doctors' warnings, unheeded when they might have done the most good, were now all that stood between a life of incarceration and execution by the state of Florida.

Proponents of capital punishment commonly argue that death penalty appeals are endless, that the same issues are litigated over and over, and that technicalities often free the most heinous murderers. It's safe to say that none of these things happened in the case of Beauford White. By the summer of 1987, he had already had his claims rejected by the state and federal courts, and he was in desperate straits.

A last-ditch effort in the federal courts was all that remained. The judge who would hear the final appeal of Beauford White was the newly appointed Stanley Marcus, fresh from heading the U.S. Attorney's Office that had indicted and convicted the lead detectives in the case.

Marcus had already denied White's appeal once, but that was before the drug conspiracy among the victims or the corruption of the investigating police officers had come to light—before the very real possibility that the main eyewitness had lied about the crime. Surely the former United States Attorney would see the significance of these new revelations, especially since the jury had voted unanimously for life without even knowing what Judge Marcus now knew.

On the night of August 25, 1987, from 4:00 p.m. to 11:00 p.m., a hearing concerning the fate of Beauford White took place in the federal courthouse in Key West, Florida. Less than twenty-four hours later, in an opinion a higher court later referred to as "carefully reasoned," Marcus made quick work of the defense arguments. Evidence that the victims were involved in drug trafficking, and that the murders were planned executions by Francois and Ferguson, had no bearing on "whether White was guilty of the first degree murder charges and whether the death penalty had been properly imposed." The fact that the main eyewitness had lied about his business in the drug house and his own involvement "was not central" to the issue of White's guilt, and "in no way" exonerated him. The subsequent criminality of many of the police officers involved in the investigation of the case—officers convicted and incarcerated by the U.S. Attorney's Office run by Marcus before he became a judge—is not mentioned at all in his thirty-five-page opinion.

The case moved quickly from there. The next day, the U.S. Supreme Court denied review; the appeals had run their course. Two justices, Brennan and Marshall, disagreed with the denial. Noting that White had been "duped into what he later discovered was a planned contract murder of one or two of the victims," that he was "visibly shaken afterwards and refused to help dispose of the weapons," and that the trial judge had disregarded the jury's unanimous recommendation, the justices argued that White's execution was "inexcusable." But they were the only two, and on August 28, 1987, Beauford White died in the Florida electric chair. Two other men, in Alabama and Utah, were executed as well, making it the first time in modern U.S. history that three men were executed on the same day.

In retrospect, Judge Marcus's opinion seems to squarely address the main issue in the case. "We are firmly convinced," Marcus wrote, "from a detailed review of the newly discovered evidence, that there is no reasonable probability that, had this evidence been disclosed to the defense, the results of the proceedings would have been any different." In other words, if the defense *had* known that the main eyewitness was lying, that the police were corrupt, that the killings were actually an orchestrated hit rather than a late decision to eliminate the witnesses—would any of it have made a difference to Judge Fuller? Was there any evidence at all that might have persuaded him to go along with the jury recommendation for a life sentence?

Perhaps not. It turns out only one other person in American history has ever been given a death sentence and then executed after a 12–0 jury recommendation of life: Bernard Bolender. After deliberating six hours and then convicting him of four murders, Bolender's jury deliberated only twelve minutes before unanimously voting for life in prison. His lawyers claimed that the jury reached its startlingly quick decision because of questions regarding Bolender's guilt. But the trial judge over-rode the jury's recommendation, imposing a death sentence, and Bolender was executed in 1995. The judge in that case? Richard S. Fuller.

In a sworn affidavit, Jimmy Della Fera, one of Bolender's lawyers, wrote that "the judge assigned to the case, the Honorable Richard S. Fuller, was predisposed to impose death and that there was not much that could be presented in the way of mitigation that would make any difference to Judge Fuller . . . I did not think it mattered much what the jury recommended because the judge had the final say. As it turned out, the jury did recommend life, and Judge Fuller overrode that recommendation and imposed death." It's possible that White's fate was sealed not when he stood by and watched six people killed, but when he was assigned to Judge Fuller's courtroom.

It took twenty-six years for the circle to close on Carol City, and for most of that time, John Errol Ferguson's lawyers argued that their client could not proceed with his appeals because he was too mentally ill to meaningfully consult with them. The Florida courts disagreed: they acknowledged that at one time he had "suffered from a mental disorder that had symptoms associated with paranoid schizophrenia," but that since 1994, his mental health had improved so as to make him "no longer a disruptive member of his prison environment." Indeed, rather than finding him overtly psychotic and too dangerous to be walking the streets, as the doctors who evaluated Ferguson before the killings had, the Florida courts concluded that his disorder was in remission and that he was malingering or exaggerating his symptoms.

This was far from the universal view of the medical community, however. Virtually every criminal trial involving a mental health opinion has expert testimony from both the prosecution and the defense, and such cases routinely devolve into a battle of experts. Ferguson's certainly did. At every one of his hearings, doctors were lined up on both sides, and more than a dozen of them concluded that he was too mentally ill to proceed. In every instance, however, the state prevailed, and slowly but inexorably his case moved toward a conclusion.

As the date of his execution neared, Ferguson's attorneys claimed that he was incompetent to be killed by the state. In other words, he was too mentally ill to rationally understand the reason he was being executed. By this time there was little talk of Ferguson being a malingerer. Everyone agreed that he was a paranoid schizophrenic with grandiose religious delusions about being the Prince of God. But the last court to take a look at his case, the Eleventh Circuit Court of Appeals, was not persuaded of his incompetence: "That most people would characterize Ferguson's Prince of God belief, in the vernacular, as 'crazy' does not mean that someone who holds that belief is not competent to be executed." On August 5, 2013, John Errol Ferguson took his last breath. His final words, spoken calmly, were, "I just want everyone to know that I am the Prince of God and will rise again."

Judicial override is not yet a thing of the past, though the main proponents of the practice—Alabama and Florida—have in recent years passed laws prohibiting it in the future. Close to three dozen people remain eligible for execution after the majority of their jurors voted for life, however; and while the Florida trial courts had not overruled a jury recommendation of life since 1999, the repercussions of the practice can still be felt today. In 2010, the United States Court of Appeals for the Eleventh Circuit upheld the override of Matthew Marshall from more than twenty years earlier, and in 2017 the Supreme

Court of Florida did as well. He remains on Florida's death row awaiting execution, along with two other Florida men who had persuaded their juries but not their judges.

Those numbers pale in comparison to Alabama, however, where the override of jury sentencing had its greatest vitality. While Florida ruled in 1975 that great weight should be given to jury recommendations (although that "great weight" had not affected Judge Fuller), its neighbor to the north declined to follow the same rule. Alabama's legal code, updated in 1981, declared, "While the jury's recommendation concerning sentence shall be given consideration, it is not binding upon the court." This resulted in eighteen death sentences just this century over the will of the jury. Other states, like Missouri and Indiana, allow judges to impose the sentence if a jury is not unanimous for life. This led to a Missouri judge in 2017 sentencing a man to death after his jury voted 11–1 for life.

And Missouri, like Florida and Alabama, elects its trial judges. This fact plays a huge, if predictable, role in sentencing outcomes. As far back as the 1930s, Alabama judge James Edwin Horton was quickly booted out of office after granting the "Scottsboro Boys" a new trial following a racist and unfounded capital rape prosecution. Since then, judges have been stressing their "law and order" bona fides at election time, and poll numbers in Alabama strongly suggest that supporting the death penalty is a vote-getter.

While judicial overrides have now ended in most states and become exceedingly rare in the rest, the Supreme Court has never outlawed the practice. The 1995 case of *Harris v. Alabama* allowed that state's override policy to stand. The sole dissenting voice belonged to Justice John Paul Stevens, who observed that capital judges may be "too responsive to a political climate in which [those] who covet higher office—or who merely wish to remain judges—must constantly profess their fealty to the death penalty." He added that the danger of judges "bend[ing] to political pressures when pronouncing sentence in highly publicized capital cases is the same danger confronted by judges beholden to King George III." Justice Stevens then noted a striking disparity: Alabama judges had vetoed only five jury recommendations of death, but had condemned forty-seven defendants whom juries would have spared. By 2011 those numbers had become even more extreme: ninety-eight overrides for death, only nine for life.

The U.S. Supreme Court hasn't issued an opinion on judge override since 1995. The case of Mario Dion Woodward nearly reached the Court in 2013, but the justices declined to hear it. Only Justices Sonia Sotomayor and Stephen Breyer objected to the denial of certiorari—Sotomayor noted that Alabama judges "appear to have succumbed to electoral pressures." The *New York Times*'s editorial board chimed in the same day, arguing that a death penalty "should not be imposed by a judge who is worried about keeping his job." Woodward tried again to reach the Supreme Court in 2019, arguing that since Alabama had outlawed the practice of judge override, his jury's 8–4 vote for life should now prevail. This time the Court ignored his request without dissent.

Whether Richard S. Fuller—who passed away in 1997—was worried about keeping his job when he overruled unanimous life recommendations would be cold comfort to Beauford White or Bernard Bolender. As for the dozens of inmates now similarly situated on death row, the Supreme Court's recent refusals to hear the Woodward case are disappointing reminders that electoral pressure on state judges is still constitutionally permissible.

But there is a fundamental injustice that must be confronted as well, summed up perfectly by Woodward's attorneys in describing the ironic despair of their client and the dozens of others: "save for an accident of timing, the life sentence imposed by a jury of their peers would have been dispositive . . . This result is as indefensible as it is unjust." For those suffering that accident of timing, it would seem that judges like Fuller are still having the last word.

2

How Crazy Is Too Crazy
to Be Executed?

Years later, after Andre Thomas had been convicted of killing his estranged wife, his four-year-old son, and her thirteen-month-old daughter in the most bizarre case in Grayson County history, after he had received a death sentence and been told that it would be imposed at the appropriate future time, after he had been dispatched to Texas's death row to wait his turn with the other condemned men and women, the prosecutors were still talking about "the eyeball issue."

Certainly there were other details that made the crime uniquely memorable. For one thing, Andre had cut out the children's hearts and returned home with the organs in his pockets. For another, he was careful to use three different knives so that the blood from each body would not cross-contaminate, thereby ensuring that the demons inside each of them would die. He then stabbed himself in the chest, but he did not die as he had hoped. In fact, he was well enough to leave a message on his wife's parents' phone explaining that he thought he was in hell, and he managed to confess to the police what he had done before they took him in for emergency surgery. The entire episode had Biblical overtones—Andre had convinced himself that his wife was Jezebel, his son the Antichrist, and her daughter just plain evil. In short, the case had enough spectacular aspects to keep the most jaded of court watchers buzzing for months, but it was the eyeball issue that garnered most of the attention. And that was only the beginning.

But the beginning of the crime is never the beginning of the story. A case like this one doesn't drop cleanly out of the sky, just as no one suddenly wakes up one day and decides to take an Uzi to the mall. Andre, who was raised in Sherman, Texas, a small town about sixty miles north of Dallas, had gnarled roots, and it was next to impossible not to trip over them. People who do capital defense work for a living like to draw family trees, because patterns of mental illness and substance abuse and domestic discord and parental neglect tend to emerge from their branches like an old Polaroid developing on the kitchen table.

Andre's family tree had all of these patterns going back two generations, and likely you could have gone back two more and found the same assortment of disabilities. This is not only true of stricken souls like Andre—take a look at the family trees of Ernest Hemingway, or the composer Robert Schumann, and you'll see manic depression and suicide running through their branches as well. But Andre's was more tortured than most. You'd have to look long and hard to find a pedigree more predictive of disaster.

Andre's grandmother, Vivian, was already a full-blown drunk by her mid-teens, so it's hardly surprising that she fell in with drunks as well. Johnny, Andre's grandfather, beat Vivian regularly, occasionally threatened to kill her with his gun, and once pushed her to the ground when she was pregnant, breaking the foot of her child in utero. Johnny was vicious but also strange—one of Vivian's children remembered the time he threw all the food in the house into the yard.

Vivian had nine children with five different men starting at the age of fourteen. After Vivian left Johnny, she married a man named Walter Martin, and the pattern continued—heavy drinking and a steady diet of domestic violence. It was in 1973, during one of their battles, that Walter put a gun to Vivian's head. Andre's uncle Gregory, who was all of seventeen at the time, tried to pull the gun away, and that's when Walter shot him in the stomach, killing him. Walter would later boast that he "planted" one of Vivian's children, and fully intended to "plant another one." Vivian's daughter Rochelle, who was closest in age to Gregory, never recovered from his killing. She, too, drank heavily, suffered from depression, and according to her siblings was sexually molested by Walter. Rochelle was Andre's mother, and that was half the genetic pie.

Andre's mostly absentee father, Danny Thomas, came from practically the same background—generational alcoholism, violence, mental illness. One of his brothers suffered from alcohol-induced dementia. Another was locked up in a state intellectual disability ward. Looking at both wings of the family side by side was like snipping away at a piece of folded paper in elementary school and opening it to find two identical sides of a snowflake.

But what did it all add up to when you stacked Andre's background against the removal of people's hearts? Alcohol, violence, mental illness, trauma—that isn't an unusual background for a death row inmate. Cable TV and criminology courses are loaded with that sort of thing. It was the eyeball issue that made people realize this was more than just the most bizarre case in Grayson County history.

Yet even the eyeball issue, like the Polaroid on the table, was a slow-developing story. It probably started with Vivian, who claimed to have a gift from God—more of a torment, really.

She believed she received divine messages through dreams and visions, only she "didn't handle the gifts," as one of her children recalled. "They handled her." Vivian saw her talent as a line that one could approach but never cross—a line separating dreams and visions from madness and delusion.

It is almost certain that Rochelle, the next generation of the gifted, crossed that line. She, too, believed that she had been chosen to hear God's messages—that her mother's gift had been passed down to her. This proved a curse for her and Andre alike. God often told Rochelle what to do, and she was certain that He was telling her son as well.

Andre was the fifth of Rochelle's six children—all boys. By the time he came along, in 1983, Rochelle had sons by three different men. She moved around constantly, and often relied on a local church to pay her utility bills. Yet despite living in one of the most chaotic situations in which a little boy might find himself, Andre somehow thrived. He received outstanding marks in kindergarten and first grade, and was placed in his school's "gifted and talented" program. His second-grade teacher described him as a "strong and delightful student."

Andre's mother, meanwhile, couldn't even say where her son went to school—as she later testified, she had so many children she simply couldn't keep track of them. This is not quite as absurd as it might sound: thanks to his mother's transience, Andre attended three different schools in three different cities in two different states, and that was just second grade.

Around third grade Andre started telling his friends, apparently in earnest, that he was Raiden, a character from the video game Mortal Kombat. Like his mother and grandmother before him, he was hearing voices. He made no secret of it. Lots of people knew that Andre suffered from what the professionals called "auditory hallucinations." At ten, he attempted suicide by slitting his wrists. He would try again three years later, sawing at his arm with a butcher knife. Both attempts were prompted by Andre's mother saying she should have aborted him.

He also began dabbling in petty crimes. When he was eleven, he was charged with criminal mischief after damaging some golf carts, and was later charged with theft for stealing a car and driving it into a ditch. He faced the consequences alone. No parent or guardian was on hand to support him when he first met with his probation officer to determine a case plan.

As Andre grew older, his grades slipped and he was forced to repeat seventh grade. He managed to climb back into the gifted and talented program, only to regress as his family life deteriorated further. When his mother told him of a plan to move the family to Oklahoma, he informed his probation officer, and a judge placed him in a juvenile detention facility. The justice system would become Andre's surrogate parent, keeping tabs on his whereabouts and overseeing his affairs. He once asked the judge for a work permit so that he could pay off his restitution and court fees, only to be told that at fourteen he was too young to work.

At age sixteen, on top of all of his other problems, Andre became a father. He had been seeing Laura Boren for several years when Little Andre came along. He dropped out of school, earned his GED, and began doing various low-wage jobs—at one point digging graves at Sherman's West Hill Cemetery. The couple found their own place for a while, but later ended up moving in with Laura's parents, and then with Andre's mother. They got married on Andre's eighteenth birthday, and Rochelle kicked them out of her house two weeks later. With nowhere they could live together, the newlyweds parted ways. Laura took Little Andre back to her parents' house and Andre moved in with his brother. After four and a half months, they separated for good.

Andre's world, already tenuous, was falling apart. He lost some seasonal work mowing grass, and struggled to pay for heat and electricity. And because his place lacked utilities, Laura began scaling back his visits with his son. Andre remarked to his father that he was in a circle he couldn't break out of.

He kept trying, though, and sought out counseling for his suicidal feelings and the voices that wouldn't keep quiet. By the time he was nineteen, they were blaring in his head like a brass band in a nightmarish parade, and he had attempted suicide several more times. As the date of the murders approached, Andre's behavior grew ever weirder. He stopped talking for days at a time, placing duct tape over his mouth. He fixated on the dollar bill, imagining a code for his salvation among its symbols.

Three weeks before the killings, he overdosed on Coricidin—a brand of cough medicine—and wound up at a mental health facility in Sherman, where he asked the staff to kill him. "Life is too much for me to handle," he said. Somehow they let him leave on his assurance that he was going straight to a nearby hospital. When he failed to show up, a warrant went out for his immediate apprehension, but the police failed to enforce it. Two days before the killings Andre overdosed again, and stabbed himself with a knife. He walked into the ER at the Texoma Medical Center, where an attending physician deemed him suicidal, and quoted him saying he was trying to "cross over into heaven."

The doctor would later testify that Andre was "really mentally ill," as if to stress that this wasn't just your run-of-the-mill crazy person. And then there was this detail from the physician's records: "Thomas," he wrote, "is psychotic. He thinks something like Holodeck on Star Trek is happening to him." If you don't know what that is, and there is no good reason you should, a holodeck is a simulated reality facility—a place where nothing is real.

Finally, the patient wanted to know whether he had volunteered for his life, or been forced to live it. Maybe that was the final straw. The doctor referred Andre to the hospital's mental health unit and filled out an emergency detention order to hold him against his will. But while staffers waited for a judge to sign the order, Andre simply wandered off. The hospital called the police, but there's no evidence that officers went looking for him at the home of Andre's mother or any of his other relatives. The next time they saw him, he was walking into the Sherman police station to confess to killing his family.

What was Andre thinking when he removed the children's hearts and placed them in his pockets to take home—along with a piece of Laura's lung, which he mistook for her heart? By his own account, he had received a message from God telling him to kill Jezebel, the Antichrist, and a related evil spirit. The only other clue was the dollar bill he had folded lengthwise and left next to his wife's leg, exposing the pyramid with the eye at the top.

Pull out a dollar bill and look at the back for yourself. Above the eye are the words *Annuit Coeptis*: "He approves our undertakings." It's likely you haven't thought much about this, but Andre did—for hours at a time. Maybe he was seeking approval, and the dollar bill served to confirm the words that kept pounding in his head. But two days later, when he was confessing his crime to the police, he called the eye at the top of the pyramid "evil." A day after that, he explained that he was the "thirteenth warrior on the dollar bill." (It just so happens that there are thirteen steps on the pyramid, for the thirteen original states, but no reference to warriors.)

A further explanation followed: according to the notes of the nurse who was monitoring Andre in his glass-walled observation cell at the Grayson County jail, his wife and kids weren't really dead. He had removed their hearts to free them from evil.

Andre refused the anti-psychotic medication the jail doctors prescribed him, but at least he had the Bible, and when he wasn't acting belligerently or gesticulating wildly or ranting about evil he would read from it. One can only wonder what he thought when he turned to Matthew 5:29—particularly in light of his obsession with the eye on the pyramid. "If your right eye causes you to sin," the passage reads, "gouge it out and throw it away. It is better for you to lose one part of your body than for your whole body to be thrown into hell." And that is precisely what Andre did. Sitting in his cell, reading the Bible, he gouged out his right eye with his fingers. Had it finally dawned on him, six days after the killings, what he had done?

There is a word for almost everything in this world, and there is a word for the intentional removal of one's own eye: auto-enucleation. What little medical literature exists on this malady states the obvious: it is an extraordinarily rare form of self-mutilation brought about by extreme psychosis. It occurs with paranoid delusions, often of a religious nature, that accompany schizophrenia, and is occasionally referred to as Oedipism.

The reference, of course, is to the myth of Oedipus the King, who blinds himself after learning that he has fulfilled a prophecy by murdering his father and sleeping with his mother. For Oedipus, it is not schizophrenia or delusions, but rather his own guilt and the merciless Fates that cause him to stab out his eyes. Yet even blinding himself can't save him: "I know death will not ever come to me through sickness or in any natural way," he laments at the end of the Sophocles play *Oedipus Rex*. "I have been preserved for some unthinkable fate."

When Andre took his eye out, the legal proceedings stopped in their tracks. Who knew what the man might say or do in front of twelve jurors? For starters, the authorities quickly equipped him with big mittens—fastened to his wrists to prevent their removal—to protect his other eye. Three doctors evaluated him—one from the jail, one appointed by the court, and one brought in by the state. All of them said that Andre suffered from some form of schizophrenia. He was declared incompetent for trial and shipped off to the secure wing of North Texas State Hospital, where he continued to hear voices and talk to himself, and seemed to have a recurring dream that scorpions and tarantulas were trying to eat him.

But this wasn't the sort of case likely to fade from public view. Maybe that was why Andre's diagnosis was changed during his stay at the state hospital. At the end of forty-seven days of evaluations and medications, the doctors concluded that most of his hallucinations were substance-induced. His discharge order seems contradictory: the doctors said Andre was malingering by exaggerating his mental illness, and yet they made him wear the mittens throughout his stay. They also noted that he was consistently cooperative with staff, behavior that is not at all typical of malingerers. Andre was now competent to stand trial, they wrote, and the court so found.

Still, the eyeball issue had gotten everybody's attention. At one point the district attorney of Grayson County had called it the desperate act of a man who feared punishment, but as the trial date approached, the prosecution seemed more circumspect. After all, the defense would surely argue that Andre was insane, and could even the most hardened DA suggest that he was faking it—that he had scooped out his own eye to manipulate the jury?

For the prosecution, one big decision remained: Would the state seek the death penalty? After all, no murder, no matter how heinous, depraved, or just plain bizarre, requires it. Ever since the Supreme Court outlawed mandatory death sentences forty-five years ago, these decisions have been left to the prosecutors. In Texas, district attorneys have used their discretion broadly, not only in seeking the death penalty but also in making sure it is carried out. The Lone Star State alone is responsible for 37 percent of all executions in the United States since 1977, when the death penalty came back into vogue.

But discretion has its limits. Race, for one, cannot be considered at all. Not to say it never is—just that it is technically unconstitutional to do so. Yet race tends to play a big role in capital cases, especially ones like the Thomas case, where the victim is white and the defendant is Black.

Laura Boren Thomas, Andre's late wife, was white. The children he killed were mixed race. These facts were particularly important when it came to jury selection. Under questioning by the lawyers, four of the twelve eventual jurors were opposed to people of mixed-race backgrounds marrying and/or having children. One even stated that he did not believe "God intended for this." Andre's court-appointed lawyers did not object, and the jurors were seated.

In fact, for this particular jury selection, the prosecutors invoked an option available only in Texas. It's called the "shuffle." The pool of potential jurors, known as a venire, are seated in a room, and with no information other than what the jurors look like, either side can request that they be shuffled—reseated in a different order.

The order of the venire, it turns out, is crucial to the jury's final makeup. That's because each juror is questioned in turn, and if lawyers from either side want to exercise their right to disqualify someone, they have to do it then and there. If it looks like one side is striking a juror based on race—which is not allowed—the other side can mount a challenge. Hence the shuffle: at Andre's trial, there were initially six African Americans seated in the first two rows. After the shuffle—which proceeded without any objection by the defense—there were no Blacks in the first five rows. Ultimately, two Black jurors were questioned and dismissed. When all was said and done, the entire jury—not to mention the judge and all of the lawyers—were white.

It's fair to say that race played a role in more than just the jury selection. The crime and the trial both took place in Sherman, a town still remembered for a shocking lynching and subsequent race riot back in 1930. In the spring of that year, a Black farmhand named George Hughes was accused of raping a young white woman. He surrendered to the police, and a trial was set for six days later.

False rumors that the woman had been mutilated spread across the town, and on the morning of trial, as many as five thousand people descended on the Grayson County courthouse hell-bent on revenge. As the trial commenced, the mob battled with state police and set the building on fire. Hughes, who had been placed in a county vault for his protection, died. The townspeople pulled his corpse into the street, dragged it behind a car, and hung it from a tree. In the mayhem that followed, most of the town's Black businesses, and one residence, were burned to the ground. The governor imposed martial law, and for two weeks the state militia took over the town. Sherman's Black community never fully recovered from the trauma—for the next sixty-five years, not a single Black doctor or lawyer practiced within its boundaries.

It was here, in Sherman, that Andre Thomas not only married a white woman, but became friends with a number of others, who showed up at the sentencing to testify on his behalf. This did not go unnoticed by the prosecutor. In the last sentence of his closing argument in favor of the death penalty, he mentioned the "string of girls that came up here," and asked the jurors if they were willing to risk Andre "asking your daughter out, or your granddaughter out?"

Statements like these tended to distract the jury from the more pressing question of Andre's mental health problems. Given the grisly details of the crime—and the eyeball incident—more than a few observers were undoubtedly left wondering just how crazy a person could be and still face execution.

There is no simple answer to this question. State courts across the country have struggled to define "intellectual disability" (formerly known as mental retardation) since 2002, when the Supreme Court ruled that intellectually disabled people are exempt from capital punishment. The high court has also banned the execution of those under eighteen at the time of their crimes, but no court has ruled that severe mental illness makes a person ineligible for the death penalty.

The Supreme Court's latest foray into the issue involved the case of Scott Louis Panetti, another Texas death row inmate. Panetti, a diagnosed schizophrenic who killed his in-laws, defended himself in court wearing a purple cowboy suit. As if that weren't enough, he asked to subpoena Jesus, John F. Kennedy, and the pope. While the justices didn't offer any clear standard on how crazy is too crazy, they suggested that severe mental illness might render someone's "perception of reality so distorted" that he could not be constitutionally executed.

As it stands, a person cannot be put to death if he or she is deemed "insane," but that's a narrow legal definition. Whether at trial or on the eve of execution, an insanity defense hinges on a defendant's inability to connect his crime with the consequences. Absent that connection, neither deterrence nor retribution is served by execution. As the legal scholar Sir William

Blackstone put it more than two hundred years ago, madness is its own punishment.

Almost every state, including Texas, now utilizes some version of what is known as the M'Naghten Rule. Daniel M'Naghten, an Englishman, was put on trial in 1843 for fatally shooting a civil servant he apparently mistook for the prime minister. He had delusions of persecution, and a number of doctors testified that he was unable to hold himself back. When the prosecution produced no witnesses to say otherwise, M'Naghten was found not guilty by reason of insanity. He spent most of the rest of his life at the State Criminal Lunatic Asylum in London's Bethlem Royal Hospital, which locals pronounced "Bedlam."

Thus was coined a word we associate with chaos—and it was chaos that ensued when M'Naghten was acquitted and the public took the verdict poorly. What emerged amid the outcry was the generally applied law that an insanity defense would only be available to someone who cannot understand the "nature and quality" of his act.

Andre's trial hinged on this very question, but with one wrinkle. In Texas, if your insanity is caused in any way by voluntary intoxication, you cannot use it as a defense. The prosecution's doctor-experts testified that Andre was well aware he was behaving wrongly, and that his crimes may have been triggered by his cough medicine overdoses, drinking, and pot smoking.

The defense called to the witness stand doctors who pointed to Andre's history of mental illness apart from any substance abuse. And hadn't the man removed his own eye?! Was the state seriously suggesting that Andre's auto-enucleation was a ruse? No. Instead, the prosecutors argued that it "was an impulsive act." They didn't dwell on it, of course. There's no requirement that attorneys have to spend lots of time talking about evidence that hurts their case. They just said it was an impulsive act, and moved on. The jury moved on with them, and Andre's insanity plea was rejected. He was found guilty and, four days later, sentenced to death. It turned out that an impulsive act, even coupled with orders from God and the removal of hearts, could not soften the punishment for murdering three in Grayson County. And so, less than a year after killing his family, Andre went off to death row.

The state's condemned live in the Allan B. Polunsky Unit, just outside of Livingston, Texas. It looks as one might imagine a death row would look—a series of imposing concrete structures surrounded by excessive razor wire and four guard towers.

The Polunsky unit didn't become death row until 1999, after a death row inmate escaped from the old facility. At the time, the Polunsky unit was called the Terrell unit, after Charles Terrell, a Dallas insurance executive and a former board chairman at the Texas Department of Criminal Justice. But when it became death row, Terrell asked to have his name removed. He was uncomfortable being associated with capital punishment because he had problems with how it was administered.

Almost a decade later, Terrell would sign a letter supporting a state moratorium on the death penalty. The letter laid out his concerns about racial fairness in some parts of Texas, the absence of DNA testing when it was possible to do it, and his opinion that life without the possibility of parole was in fact *more* punitive for young offenders than a death sentence. He added that he was the only person he knew of who had requested that his name be removed from a building. Documents generated by the prison system in the Thomas case, however, still read "facility POLUNSKY (formerly TERRELL)." In one final touch of irony, Terrell was born in Sherman.

Death row is not designed for rehabilitation. There are no programs to attend, no degrees to obtain. The main business carried on is waiting. Those lucky enough to come to the row mentally intact may be able to hold themselves together through the years of aloneness by reading, talking to prisoners in nearby cells, or listening to the radio. But inmates like Andre, who are already debilitated by mental illness, do not get better. There are no avenues for it. The cells at Polunsky are smaller than a basketball free-throw lane, the prisoners are on lockdown more than 90 percent of the time, and there is no human contact at all. Andre still wore the mittens to protect his remaining eye, and his meals were brown-bag because he couldn't be trusted with utensils. He was taking the same medication he had been taking at the state hospital.

His diagnosis on death row, paranoid schizophrenia, was not the diagnosis prosecutors had argued to the jury that put him there, but the prison records said "no stop date indicated" for his medication. In short, the DAs could argue whatever they wanted to avoid an insanity verdict, but this guy was, as they sometimes say in Texas, "crazy as a peach-orchard boar," and prison officials were going to treat him as such.

Every once in a while there were skeptics. Like the doctor who didn't trust Andre's hallucinations because the voices always told him to "do things he wants to do anyway. People who have hallucinations do not recognize they are hallucinations." Prisons, of course, are houses of skepticism. Consider this entry from an early psychological intake form: "R eyelid is in a fixed, closed position. R eye seems to be missing (as pt claims)." Apparently the mittens weren't enough of a giveaway. And so it went from March 2005 to the summer of 2008— lots of complaints from Andre about the voices, an attempt at cutting himself with a razor blade, and the periodic suggestion that he was faking the whole thing. Mostly, though, the prison records depict a barely-getting-by paranoid schizophrenic who knows he is seriously mentally ill but doesn't have any idea what to do about it. Sometimes the voices would scream at him to "bash my head," as he put it. Other times he thought six-inch demons were coming out of the walls and playing music by the rock group Queen. And then there were days that he said he felt fine and was writing music for his mother.

On July 14, 2008, Andre managed to procure something sharp and slash a seven-centimeter gash in his throat, requiring eight stitches. He insisted that he was the cause of all the problems in the world, and that if he killed himself all the problems would stop. The next day, he reported that he had been reading his Bible and got confused because he wasn't sure if it was the voices or his own thoughts that were telling him to kill himself. During a psychiatric assessment one week later, he explained that "[t]he government is conspiring to read my mind. That's why I ripped out my right eye. That's the righteous side. They can't hear my thoughts no more. I cut my throat. Gotta shed a little blood to save the world. Like the guy in the dayroom told me, 'Don't lighten up, tighten up!'"

Prison officials were concerned enough to send him to the system's psychiatric facility, but they returned him to his regular cell within a month. It was only eight stitches, and he clearly could have inflicted far more damage.

Then again, maybe the episode signaled the start of another slide. After three years on the row, there was little question that Andre was getting worse. Or maybe it's more accurate to say that events were beginning to recur. Andre had always believed in what we all call déjà vu—except he was convinced that he was reliving days and weeks in their totality. A year prior to the killings, he complained to friends that life kept repeating itself. And since things were happening over and over again, it meant they weren't really happening at all. Shortly after his crime, when he explained to the nurse that his wife and children weren't really dead, he had said, "This is déjà vu from all reality."

By the late fall of 2008, Andre was acting much as he had in the weeks leading up to the crime. He felt suicidal again and asked for help, but refused to take his meds. He stopped talking and wouldn't eat. He came out to see his lawyer with Scotch tape clumsily covering his mouth, and insisted on writing his answers to her questions on a glass partition with his finger. It's conceivable that Andre's relapse was related to an incident in late November, when he found himself in a cell next to an inmate who swore he was the Antichrist. This enraged Andre, who believed he had already done God's work in removing the Antichrist from the earthly realm.

Perhaps what he did next—the thing that got everybody's attention again—resulted from a combination of all these things: on December 9, 2008, Andre ripped out his left eye. His only eye. And he ate it.

As he explained some days later, he didn't want the government to read his thoughts, so he ate the eye because he was certain they would figure out some way to put it back in. He said he had been reading the Book of Revelations, and felt sympathy for the devil because it wasn't all Satan's fault. After all, he was supposed to have been aborted.

After the second eye removal, it was clear that the Polunsky unit was no longer the appropriate home for Andre. He was packed off to Jester IV, a state prison psychiatric unit. As the name implies, Jester IV is one of a series of Jester units, all located in Richmond, Texas, just southwest of Houston. The complex is surrounded by cornfields. Indeed, the property once hosted the Harlem Plantation, which became a prison farm in the late 1800s. It was renamed in honor of former governor Beauford H. Jester, who served from 1946 to 1949, and was in the process of reforming the state prisons when he died in office of a heart attack.

There are a few other death row inmates at Jester IV, but the unit is reserved for the mentally ill. Andre is still locked in a small cell twenty-three hours a day, but by all accounts Jester IV is a quieter place. He seems more comfortable around other mentally ill prisoners, and he does not believe, as he did at Polunsky, that they are scheming against him. He hasn't yet learned to read Braille, and the medicine he is on now tends to knock him out for large portions of the day. While he is awake he often breaks into song. He is a big fan of Depeche Mode.

Joe Brown, the district attorney of Grayson County, said he was surprised to hear that Andre had removed his second eye, but he did not call it a second impulsive act. He simply announced that the state would gather together Andre's records and evaluate the situation.

The records themselves are remarkable if only to show how acceptable bizarre thoughts can become in a prison psychiatric setting. Eight days after swallowing his remaining eye, for example, Andre reports that he is hearing voices, including that of God, and says the government has the eye he didn't eat and he wants it back. The evaluation form accompanying these remarks indicates that he is not presenting delusional or paranoid symptoms, and that his "insight/judgment" is fair. Other records are similarly disingenuous.

Thirteen years have passed since the second eyeball incident, but Andre's prosecutors have not reported back about their record-gathering or any subsequent evaluation. Texas continues to pursue Andre's execution. No state authority figure has expressed hesitation about ending the life of a man who intentionally blinded himself, nor has there been any move by the district attorney to reconsider Andre's mental state at the time of the killings.

The only one who has revisited the issue, apart from the lawyers who are now appealing his sentence in the Texas federal courts, is Andre himself. He spoke about it with a nurse shortly after he slashed his own throat—back when he still had one eye to see with: "I killed my wife and two kids," he said. "My wife was Jezebel. God told me to, so I cut out their hearts. I fucked up though: I heard another voice. I thought it was God, so I listened. It told me not to complete the ritual and don't burn the hearts. So, I threw them out." This failure, he explained, would bring consequences: "Before 2012, they will come back and be mad I killed them."

But now it is 2021. His family hasn't come back, and won't. Andre Thomas remains in his tiny cell on death row, waiting. And no one, not even Andre, is quite certain what he is waiting for.

3

Racist and Proud (and a Judge)

You've got to be taught to hate and fear, you've got to be taught from year to year, it's got to be drummed in your dear little ear, you've got to be carefully taught.

—Oscar Hammerstein

Courts have spoken in aspirational tones about the comportment of the judiciary for hundreds of years, and with good reason. The first federal officer to be impeached and removed from office was Judge John Pickering, who had been appointed by George Washington in 1795 but by the early 1800s had developed a reputation for "ravings, cursings, and crazed incoherences." Over the years judges have been convicted of fixing cases, taking kickbacks to fill a juvenile detention facility, wire fraud, and bribery; they have slept through trials and had affairs with prosecutors and sent racist and misogynist emails to other judges, prosecutors, and defense attorneys. One traffic court judge solicited funds for his election by promising to "hook up" contributors if they appeared before him. Given such examples and many others, it is little surprise the second Justice Harlan said that "[w]e should be especially scrupulous in seeing to it that the right to a fair trial has not been jeopardized by the conduct of a member of the judiciary."

But misconduct over a traffic ticket is a far cry from bias in a death penalty prosecution, and it was just such a claim that came to the Texas courts in 2018. The "Texas Seven" case, with its own nickname, the drama of a prison escape, and the horror of a police killing, was the highest-profile crime in the state since the mass killings by Charles Whitman at the University of Texas tower in 1966. Seven men broke out of the maximum-security John B. Connally Unit of the Texas Department of Criminal Justice in mid-December 2000, killed Officer Aubrey Hawkins in a robbery of a sporting goods store outside Dallas on Christmas Eve, and somehow made it to a trailer park in southern Colorado. For three weeks the men quietly blended in with the rural community by posing as traveling missionaries, until an appearance on *America's Most Wanted* led to their apprehension. Each of the escapees had a separate trial, and over the next seventeen years three of them (one had committed suicide rather than be captured in Colorado) were executed by the state of Texas. Next up was Joseph Garcia. His fate, and that of the other two death row inmates, took a dramatic turn in May 2018 when a story broke in the *Dallas Morning News*. Not about newly discovered evidence, or prosecutorial misconduct, or even a significant legal error—rather, the article concerned Vickers Cunningham, the judge for five of the "Texas Seven" jury trials: "White, Straight and Christian: Dallas County Candidate Admits Rewarding His Kids if They Marry Within Race." The controversy about who his children married turned out to be the thin edge of the wedge.

Like many judges, Vickers Cunningham started his legal career as a prosecutor. He had grown up in Dallas, and went to work in that city's office only a few years after the longtime district attorney, Henry Wade, stepped down in 1987. Wade had run the office since 1951, and Cunningham reflected on his death in 2006: "I was Henry Wade's paperboy, and I went to school with his daughter . . . I was so impressed with Henry Wade and his legend." There is little doubt that legend was tarnished, however; first in a series of articles in the *Dallas Morning News* a year before Wade's retirement, and then nationally in two Supreme Court opinions in the early 2000s. The bottom line was this: Wade had run an office that formalized a policy to exclude minorities from jury service. As the Supreme Court noted in *Miller-El v. Cockrell* in 2003:

> A 1963 circular by the [Dallas] District Attorney's Office instructed its prosecutors to exercise peremptory strikes against minorities:
> "'Do not take Jews, Negroes, Dagos, Mexicans or a member of any minority race on a jury, no matter how rich or how well educated.'"
> . . . A manual entitled "Jury Selection in a Criminal Case" was distributed to prosecutors. It contained an article authored by a former prosecutor (and later a judge) under the direction of his superiors in the District Attorney's Office, outlining the reasoning for excluding minorities from jury service. Although the manual was written in 1968, it remained in circulation until 1976, if not later . . .

Whether or not Cunningham condoned such a policy when he worked at the office is an open question, but in 1992 he was accused of keeping Black jurors off the jury in a murder trial. He claimed that he wasn't paying attention to race; rather, he was getting rid of Democrats.

Cunningham may have learned from Wade, but he was

influenced by another famous Dallasite as well. The Reverend W. A. Criswell, leader of the largest Southern Baptist congregation in the country, had long been Cunningham's pastor and was close enough with him to officiate at his wedding. For years Criswell had preached segregation, calling integration the work of "outsiders" in "dirty shirts" who, if not stopped, would "get in your family." Christians had to "stick to their own kind," he preached, adding Catholics to his list of enemies when Kennedy ran for president in 1960. In later years he renounced his opposition to integration, turning his hostility to feminism and gay rights and other assaults on the "traditional family." When Criswell passed in 2002, Cunningham recessed one of the Texas Seven jury trials to attend the funeral.

After leaving the DA's office, Cunningham became a lower-level judge in the Dallas criminal court system. Six years later, when he was chosen by Governor Rick Perry for a promotion to the Judicial District Court, his first assignment was the trial of Donald Newbury, one of the escapees. "I felt the weight of the process on my shoulders," Cunningham said. "My first death penalty trial, with no lead-time to prepare, and to do the sentencing live [on TV] . . . I didn't sleep. I want to be sure I'm doing the best job and being fair."

The judge worked his way through three more Texas Seven trials before getting to the Randy Halprin case in 2003. There was no question of Halprin's guilt: while he denied firing a shot at the police officer, his admission to voluntarily participating in the armed robbery was enough to get him convicted. But this was a capital trial, and Halprin was fighting for his life. He presented evidence that he was the youngest of the seven and the least intelligent, and that he had no past experience with guns or any history of robberies. He also wanted to introduce a report compiled by the Texas Department of Criminal Justice, which had done its own investigation of the prison break—speaking with correctional officers, civilian workers, and inmates who worked closely with the escapees—and determined that Halprin was the least likely of the seven to have led the escape or the robbery:

> 7. Halprin was quiet and never exhibited leadership qualities. Was consistently worried about whether his work was acceptable to the civilian workers. Very submissive characteristic. This worrisome attitude was seen to escalate a month before the escape. One civilian worker speculated whether Halprin was undergoing some type of depression.

Judge Cunningham did not allow that document to be shown to the jury. Judges have wide latitude in decisions such as the admission of evidence, and appeals courts will rarely rule that a judge has abused his discretion when it comes to disallowing evidence, even in a capital case. Whether Cunningham's decision affected Halprin's sentence would be the subject of future appeals; but like all of the other escapees, Halprin went to death row. It was June 2003.

Judges make discretionary decisions in every trial, and as long as those decisions don't lie "outside the zone of reasonable disagreement," they are upheld on appeal. This rule is based on the presumption that judges are knowledgeable about the law and make their decisions in good faith. Certainly the Texas Court of Criminal Appeals did not doubt the good faith of the judge when it affirmed Halprin's conviction and death sentence in 2005. Indeed, the Court of Criminal Appeals affirmed all five of the capital cases in which he had presided. Each had resulted in a death sentence; but the first trial, handled by a different judge, had as well. There was no reason to believe that Judge Cunningham had put his thumb on the scale of justice.

Over the next thirteen years, as the Halprin case wound through the courts on its way to what seemed an inevitable conclusion, the other Texas Seven escapees—Rodriguez, Rivas, Newbury—met their fate in the Texas death chamber. Joseph Garcia's life seemed likely to end there as well; but the May 2018 article in the *Dallas Morning News* altered the arc of that case, and those that would follow. Bill Cunningham had broken the story, motivated by the fact that his brother Vickers was running for Dallas County Commissioner: "[My brother's] views and his actions are disqualifying for anyone to hold public office in 2018. It frightens me to death to think of people in power who could hurt people."

What views did he think his brother possessed that were disqualifying? Brother Bill had a long list: bigotry, racism, homophobia, hostility to non-Christians. His perspective was not universal, but rather deeply personal. He was gay and married to a Black man, a man his brother repeatedly referred to as "your boy." When Bill returned to Texas from California, Vic invited him over to share a bottle of wine, but not with his husband: "you can't bring him, he's not coming in my house." And then there was Vic's longtime nickname for his brother, "N-word Bill." Except that he didn't say "n-word."

Vickers Cunningham denied it all, and he got support from his other two brothers, who claimed that Bill had sabotaged his brother's campaign for commissioner because he'd been ousted from the family and written out of their parents' wills. They attributed Bill's anger to the fact that Vic had refused his brother a $45,000 loan. All of which may or may not have been true, but hardly explained the considerable evidence that Cunningham was in fact a racist. There was the living trust he had created to preclude a distribution if his children did not marry a white Christian of the opposite sex, a trust he defended by noting his strong support for "traditional family values." Then there was a text by Cunningham's son, later denied, about the son's relationship with a Vietnamese woman and the hope that his father might slowly "turn around"—"And if he doesn't, he will have one less person at his dinner table." A woman named Amanda Tackett, who had worked on Cunningham's campaign for district attorney in 2006, claimed that he described criminal cases involving Black people as "T.N.D.s," which stood for "Typical [N-word] Deals." It was more than enough to raise the antennae of the lawyers trying to stop the execution of Joseph Garcia. Their claim was elemental: "Because Garcia was tried before a judge who harbored racial animus toward nonwhites, Garcia was denied the fair trial before an impartial tribunal . . . guaranteed him . . . by the U.S. Constitution."

Such a claim had considerable support in Supreme Court jurisprudence. "Discrimination on the basis of race, odious in all aspects, is especially pernicious in the administration of justice," the Court had written in the 1979 case of *Rose v. Mitchell.* In the two decades before Garcia's pending execution, the Court had three times denounced racism in the jury selection process, each a capital case that had resulted in a death sentence. In two separate opinions in 2017 the Court had condemned a racist juror and a mental health expert who testified that Blacks were inherently more dangerous because of their skin color. The field had been tilled for a legal challenge to a racist judge.

Yet Garcia's claim barely made a ripple in the courts. The state's response was absurd almost to the point of naivete:

The news article cited by Garcia reflects that Cunningham set up the living trust for his children in 2010, seven
years after Garcia's trial in this case. Garcia presents no
evidence that the views discussed in the article, which
form the basis of his current complaint, existed at the
time of his trial in 2003.

That Cunningham was a racist at the age of forty-eight but not
at the age of forty-one required a suspension of disbelief, but
apparently that was the rationale the Texas courts accepted.
Joseph Garcia was executed on December 4, 2018.

When a public official is accused of misconduct in a very public
way, no one is surprised if further evidence of similar misconduct surfaces. The *Morning News* story was a bombshell in the
Dallas community—the newspaper withdrew their endorse-
ment of him for commissioner, the Republican Party rebuked
him for alleged "racist behavior and language"—and it wasn't
long before others came forward to confirm that Cunningham's
bigotry was long-standing. The fulcrum of the corroboration
was the man next scheduled for a Texas Seven execution, Randy
Halprin. As fate would have it, he happened to be Jewish.

There had been no mention of anti-Semitism in the scandal that erupted around Cunningham's campaign, but it was
hardly a leap to think that a man responsible for a white straight
Christian trust might have other concerning views as well. The
evidence soon made it clear that he did. Amanda Tackett, who
had been widely quoted in the original *Morning News* article,
pulled no punches when Halprin's lawyers came to talk to her:

I personally heard Vic refer to Mexicans as "wetbacks,"
Catholics as "idol-worshippers," Jews as "dirty" and
African-Americans as "[n-words]." . . . Around the time

Vic's campaign was gearing up for the primary, the Innocence Project began looking into cases in the Dallas-Fort Worth area. I heard Vic call Barry Scheck, the Innocence Project's co-founder, a "filthy Jew" who was going to free all the "[n-words]." . . . He continued that they are all on death row for a reason. He said, "My job is to prevent the [n-words] from running wild again."

Cunningham's anti-Semitism, like the racism and homophobia aimed at his brother's husband, reached into his own family. A Jewish man named Michael Samuels told Halprin's attorneys that Cunningham's daughter Suzy had been forced to break up with him under the threat that her father would not pay her law school tuition. "At first she tried to say that we had drifted apart as a couple," Samuels said. "But she told me that her father did not like me because I was Jewish."

The question remained: While Cunningham hated Jews, African Americans, Catholics, Mexicans, and who knows who else, did his prejudice have anything to do with the way he conducted the Texas Seven trial of Randy Halprin? Amanda Tackett thought so. She had a specific memory of Cunningham discussing the case when he was running for Dallas district attorney. "During my time in the campaign office, I heard Vic say . . . that he was anointed by God to preside over the Texas Seven trials . . . Vic referred to Mr. Halprin as 'the Jew' and others in the Texas Seven as 'wetbacks.' He then launched into his campaign speech about immigration and the importance of White people in the Dallas community." Years later, after Cunningham had lost the race for district attorney and was running for commissioner, his campaign literature was still bragging about having presided over the Texas Seven, and that he had "put more criminals on Death Row than almost any other judge in the nation."

But it took longtime family friend Tammy McKinney to put an even finer point on the connection between the ex-judge, the high-profile case, and the ethnicity of the defendants:

> I have always known Vic to tout with pride his role in the Texas Seven trials. I would go so far as to say it was his claim to fame . . . Vic took special pride in the death sentences because they included Latinos and a Jew. I did not know which one was Jewish, but Vic would tell me the guy was a "fucking Jew."

Thus had Halprin made a compelling case that a biased judge presided over his trial. Now it was up to the courts. The same courts that had remained silent while the state of Texas executed Joseph Garcia.

Capital appeals follow a consistent pattern after a death sentence: they wind through the state courts and then the federal ones, often ending in the U.S. Supreme Court, where cases are routinely ignored without so much as a comment. When executions loom, however, those patterns are disrupted; and as Halprin's time drew near, his legal team filed a flurry of petitions in every court they could find. It was the Fifth Circuit Court of Appeals, the second-highest court in the land, that first dealt with the issue of judge as bigot.

A defendant entering federal court with a death sentence must find his way through a thicket of obstacles before a court even looks at the merits of his claim. Primary among these obstacles is the law's heavy-handed attempt—via a statute designed to make the death penalty "effective"—to confine defendants to a single appeal. This was Halprin's biggest problem—he'd already had, and lost, a federal appeal. Of course, Cunningham's racism and anti-Semitism hadn't become public until several years after Halprin's federal appeal had been denied; surely the law would not protect a judge who kept his discrimination hidden while presiding over such a high-profile trial.

But not so fast. While the Fifth Circuit was quick to condemn the judge's bias ("Assuming the allegations to be true, Cunningham's racism and bigotry are horrible and completely inappropriate for a judge"), the criticism hardly jumped off the page—you had to read a footnote in the opinion to find it. The denunciation of Cunningham wasn't the end of it, though. Since this was Halprin's second federal appeal, he had to explain why he hadn't complained about the judge's bigotry before this. The seemingly obvious answer—that his bias was not public until the story broke in the *Dallas Morning News*, and thus could not have been part of the original appeal—was wrong according to the Fifth Circuit. Its reasoning was a bit more arcane: if, as Halprin claimed, his judge had been a bigot during his trial, then the claim could have been raised during his first appeal, whether Halprin knew of the bigotry or not. This was exactly the opposite of the rationale used to execute Joseph Garcia: while Garcia failed to establish Cunningham's prejudice at the time of his trial, Halprin had lost precisely because he had. Was his execution next?

The only court higher than the Fifth Circuit was the Supreme Court, and given his options Halprin had no reason not to seek intervention there. But any appeal to the highest court was a Hail Mary at best, and while his lawyers prepared to argue the illogic of the Circuit's opinion, Halprin's last best hope lay elsewhere, in a court that had previously denied two of his earlier applications.

The Texas Court of Criminal Appeals had affirmed hundreds of death sentences over the years, and Texas's lengthy execution record justified its reputation as the most bloodthirsty of states. But Halprin had the grisly advantage of having lived longer than Joseph Garcia, and thus was able to benefit from the state's acknowledgment in the *Garcia* case that Cunningham's bigotry had been hidden from the public. Perhaps it was this concession that persuaded the Dallas District Attorney's Office to remain silent on Halprin's request that his execution be stayed. In any case, with an execution date in October 2019 less than a week away, the highest Texas criminal court stayed Halprin's execution and sent the case back to a lower court for further consideration of his central claim: Would Texas allow the execution of a Jewish man whose trial was conducted by an anti-Semitic judge?

With Halprin's life no longer hanging by a thread, it was easy to forget that his appeal was still pending in the Supreme Court, and easier still when the Court went months longer than it normally would before denying review. But the denial came with an augury of optimism in the form of a short opinion by Justice Sotomayor, who felt the need to explain why she hadn't dissented in the face of "deeply disturbing" facts and "potent arguments" by Halprin. "[S]tate court proceedings are underway to address—and, if appropriate, to remedy—Halprin's assertion that insidious racial and religious bias infected his trial," she wrote. Noting that due process requires a fair trial in a fair tribunal, she concluded: "I trust that the Texas courts considering Halprin's case are more than capable of guarding this fundamental guarantee." As if to say that we'd all be watching.

4

Sex-Shamed to Death

It was July 2004 in Oklahoma City, and Brenda Andrew was on trial for killing her husband. The prosecutor had been speaking for two and a half hours, and he was wrapping up the closing argument by reading from Rob Andrew's diary about his wife's infidelity: "The first time was when I drove to her school in Kansas to surprise her and I found out she had spent the night in her old boyfriend's dorm room. Second time was during the summer when she was teaching at summer camp she met a new boyfriend and then kept dating him on the side while we were engaged." The prosecutor announced that the date of the diary entry was 1984, seventeen years before the crime. But there was no objection from the defense, and no one questioned the relevance of the passage. The jury started deliberating only a few minutes later. The following day they returned with a guilty verdict.

The conviction was not a surprise, as the evidence against her was considerable. But the jury's work was not done—their next decision was whether Brenda Andrew should live or die.

* * *

Only once in American history have three women been executed by the same state in the same year—Oklahoma in 2001. To understand the odds against such an occurrence, consider that women are arrested for about 10 percent of the homicides in the United States, but make up less than 2 percent of death row. An even smaller percentage actually lose their lives at the hands of the state.

A number of theories have been proposed to explain the bias against executing women. Richard Dieter, the former head of the Death Penalty Information Center, puts it simply: "jurors just see women differently than men." He believes that most juries are inclined to consider homicides committed by women as crimes of passion, and likely influenced by the high rate of domestic violence against women. Such cases are rarely considered appropriate for capital punishment. Law professor Victor Streib, a well-known historian of the death penalty, sees the disparity in death sentencing from a slightly different perspective: "It's just easier to convince a jury that women suffer from emotional distress or other emotional problems more than men."

Such thinking extends beyond capital punishment, since studies show women are less likely than men to be incarcerated for comparable crimes. But what explains the death sentences that are imposed on women? Professor Streib and other academics have postulated the "evil woman" theory—that women who violate society's beliefs about female behavior lose the protection that femininity typically affords them before juries, and thus subject themselves to punishments ordinarily reserved for men. This is not a new theory. In nineteenth-century England a female awaiting execution was referred to as "the wretched woman."

The Puritan ethos of moral condemnation had landed on America's shore hundreds of years earlier. This was perhaps best described by Nathaniel Hawthorne in *The Scarlet Letter*, in which he wrote of Hester Prynne with the bright red *A* "so fantastically embroidered and illuminated upon her bosom. It had the effect of a spell, taking her out of the ordinary relations with humanity, and enclosing her in a sphere by herself." But Hawthorne's novel was about sexual transgression, not murder. Today the hypocrisy—that we are more likely to harshly condemn women who violate sexual mores and less likely to sentence female murderers to death—might seem anachronistic. The combination of sexual impropriety and murder is still a very potent mix, however.

Two days after the jury convicted Brenda Andrew of her husband's murder, they sentenced her to death. This was not a foregone conclusion; the great majority of murder convictions do not end in death sentences. How the prosecution sent her to death row is a matter of record, a page torn from the same demonizing playbook demagogues have relied on from Biblical times through the 2021 Twitter feed. That the courts have looked the other way—and pushed Brenda Andrew closer to execution by doing so—is a testament to the continuing viability of the "evil woman" theory, and the ingrained sexism that persists as an acceptable and even legal veneer.

Parishioners at the North Pointe Baptist Church in Edmond, Oklahoma, are pretty much the same as everybody else—if they see people acting differently than they believe they should act, they whisper about it. Certainly Brenda Andrew drew her share of whispers at the church she and her husband attended. She was a very pretty woman who favored short, tight dresses. She flirted with men who did work around her house. She once changed the color of her hair after learning that a man she liked was partial to redheads. And she slept with men other than her husband.

Her final affair, with a man named James Pavatt, led to both of them being convicted of murder. They had met in 1999 when both became members of the church. Soon they were teaching a Sunday school class together. Pavatt sold insurance, and, like a character in a 1930s potboiler, had arranged a life insurance policy for Rob Andrew worth $800,000. Brenda was the policy's beneficiary.

The Pavatt and Andrew families went to dinners and Bible study with each other, and it wasn't long before James and Brenda came together, and both families came apart. In the summer of 2001, Pavatt got divorced, and all that whispering started at the church. Just a few months later, Rob moved out of his home, and the Andrews began their own divorce proceedings soon after. The elders asked them to stop teaching the Sunday school class.

Maybe it was the money, maybe it was the attraction, but as the late summer turned to fall it wasn't hard to imagine that blood might be spilled. In October someone cut the brake lines on Rob Andrew's car, which prompted him to accuse Brenda and Pavatt of trying to kill him. Not surprisingly, he tried to remove his wife as the beneficiary of his life insurance policy. At her trial, the state presented evidence that before the brake lines had been cut, she and Pavatt had attempted to change the ownership of the policy from Rob to Brenda by forging Rob's signature. As in all murder cases, things were coming to a head.

On November 20, 2001, Rob Andrew died from two shotgun blasts in the garage of the family home. He had gone there to pick up his two young children for a Thanksgiving vacation, but he never made it to the living room, where the children were watching television (at a louder volume than normal, the prosecution argued). Brenda was with her estranged husband in the garage, and suffered a superficial gunshot wound to her arm. Evidence suggested that the injury was not caused by a shotgun, and was from close range, which contradicted her claim that two masked gunmen had shot them both from a distance. Attention almost immediately focused on her and Pavatt as the perpetrators. Before her husband's funeral, Brenda fled to Mexico with Pavatt and her children. Both of them were charged with murder before the month ended. By late February of the next year they had run out of money, and they were taken into custody crossing back into the United States.

It was not long after Brenda's arrest that the press began categorizing her as a woman who slept around. An article entitled "Church and Fate," published in *People* magazine seven months after her arrest, quoted one of Rob Andrew's colleagues: "One time we were driving by a motel and Rob casually told me he found Brenda at the motel with a former boyfriend after he was engaged to her. I said, 'Rob, wake up.'" The same article referenced two prior affairs she'd had before she and Pavatt "began to carry on like teenagers that summer, giggling and passing notes during [church] services."

Pavatt's 2003 trial, which came six months before Andrew's, previewed the trial against her. Indeed, the evidence against him was in many ways identical to that facing his co-defendant. There was the relationship between the two of them, the attempted manipulation of the insurance policy, and the flight to Mexico. Pavatt's own adult daughter testified about the affair between her father and Brenda. And there was one other crushing piece of evidence against Pavatt—a letter allegedly written by him to Brenda's daughter accepting blame for the murder and exonerating Brenda. But while the state introduced the letter into evidence, both sides contested its veracity, the prosecution claiming it only told half the story while the defense suggested Pavatt hadn't written it at all. It didn't matter. Pavatt was convicted and sentenced to death.

The Pavatt trial also proved to be a dress rehearsal for the "evil woman" theory that was going to dominate Brenda's trial. One of her ex-lovers, a man named Higgins, was called by the prosecution to testify that she had once told him she wished her husband dead for her own financial benefit. But the state's questioning of Higgins, which was largely repeated at her trial as well, strayed far from the question of guilt:

Q: Where did you first meet Brenda Andrew?
A: I met her in a grocery store. I was working there and she came in.
Q: And how did you meet her?
A: Basically I was working there and she came in and was flirting, being friendly. And I just talked to her and made her acquaintance.
Q: What do you mean she was flirting?
A: She was just being friendly and came in dressed real sexy looking, short dresses, and that sort of thing. And just came on to me and I just reacted to it.
Q: And did you believe when she came in there and was flirting with you that she was coming on to you?
A: Yes, I did.
Q: No doubt in your mind?
A: None.
Q: As a result of her coming on to you did you then form a relationship with her?
A: Yes, I did.
Q: Were you a married man?
A: Yes.
Q: And did you have knowledge that Brenda Andrew was married as well?
A: Yes.
[. . .]

Q: How long did this flirtatiousness continue between you and Brenda Andrew before the relationship became more serious?

A: Till about March and at that time she came into the store and handed me . . . stuck her hand out to hand me something and I put my hand out and it was a key to a motel room. And she said meet me there when you get off work.

Q: Did you do that?

A: Yes, I did.

[. . .]

Q: Who paid for that motel?

A: She did.

[. . .]

Q: And without going into any detail, when you all went to the motel did you have a sexual relationship?

A: Yes, we did.

Q: Did that sexual relationship with Brenda Andrew continue for a period of time?

A: Yes, it did.

Q: How long?

A: Till May of the next year.

Q: So approximately—

A: Little over a year, yes.

Q: Little over a year? Now, during this year and a little over a year period of time that you were having a relationship with Brenda Andrew, did you always go to a motel?

A: Most of the time, yes.

Q: Were there other places where you went to meet her to have sex?

A: Her car.

Q: And did Brenda always pay for the motel room?
A: Almost all the time, maybe once or twice she didn't.

Then there was the search warrant of Brenda's home, which yielded a long list of items, among them microcassette answering machine tapes, insurance documents, financial paperwork, and a few handwritten notes. But one item stood out. Among the many certificates and reports, the prosecution introduced into evidence a book found in the middle drawer of her bedroom dresser: *203 Ways to Drive a Man Wild in Bed.*

You might ask why the prosecution felt the need to paint Brenda Andrew in scarlet, when the evidence against her was virtually the same as against Pavatt, for whom they had already obtained a death sentence. But the death penalty, and who gets it, is not subject to an algorithm. Serial murderers like Washington State's Green River Killer, the Unabomber, and the Kansas BTK Killer are serving multiple life sentences after plea bargains, while those who choose to go to trial having committed far less egregious crimes often end up executed or on death row.

Nor are juries predictable when it comes to ascertaining who deserves the harshest punishment. Courthouse killer Brian Nichols avoided a death sentence in 2008 after killing a judge, a court reporter, a deputy sheriff, and a federal agent after escaping during his trial for rape. James Holmes, who killed twelve and injured more than seventy in an Aurora movie theater, went to trial in 2015 and will die a natural death as well.

Such capricious results have been extensively noted at the highest levels: Supreme Court Justice Stewart declared death sentences "cruel and unusual in the same way that being struck by lightning is" in 1972. Two decades later Supreme

Court Justice Blackmun famously announced that he would no longer "tinker with the machinery of death" for much the same reason; and Justice Breyer catalogued the arbitrariness in a lengthy dissent in 2015.

While there is no formula to predict who will or won't get a death sentence, statisticians would have no trouble drawing conclusions about the impact of gender on Oklahoma's death penalty. Of its two hundred executions since statehood, only the three from 2001 were women. No woman since Brenda Andrew has been sentenced to death in Oklahoma, and she is currently the only woman among the forty-seven people on death row. Pavatt and Andrew might have committed the same crime, but there is little doubt that Pavatt was far more likely to receive a death sentence. Whether consciously or not, the prosecution surely understood that obtaining a death sentence for Brenda Andrew was going to require more than a straightforward presentation of relevant evidence regarding the murder of her husband.

But more what? The literature examining the intersection of gender and criminology is replete with examples of behavior that violates stereotypes of female norms and expectations. Modern feminist theorists refer to this as "double deviance": the punishment of women for their crimes and for their lack of conformity to female gender expectations. When women are portrayed as violent, masculine, or victimizers of children, they are more likely to be considered "evil women" and condemned for criminality. Perhaps the most common deviation from stereotypically acceptable feminine behavior in our society is promiscuity, and the prosecution had more than enough evidence of that.

It didn't take long for them to use it, either. The second sentence of the state's opening statement identified Pavatt as "one of her lovers." Shortly after that, the prosecutor declared that "Brenda had extracurricular activities. She liked to cheat on Rob . . . throughout the marriage Brenda had a boyfriend on the side." Before her trial was over, the jury learned that Brenda was "coming on" to Higgins's sons, who were helping to build a deck at her house; that when she appeared in a restaurant dressed in a revealing manner, someone from the bar asked who the "hoochie" was; and that her babysitter from several years before the crime had a problem with her choice of clothes:

A: [Brenda] was going to run, get some groceries and do some other errands.

Q: Is that what she told you?

A: Yes.

Q: Did you notice anything at that point that you thought was unusual in regards to what she just told you?

A: Yes. She wasn't wearing attire that I would consider appropriate for running errands. She had on a leather—

Defense Attorney: Objection, Judge, as to what this witness thinks is appropriate or not appropriate. Judge, it's not being relevant to any issue that we're here on in this case.

The Court: Overruled. Go ahead.

The Witness: Okay. It was a leather outfit. It was a leather skirt and leather button-up top and she had rolled her hair and it was really, really big . . .

There was even speculation from Pavatt's own daughter that her father had not likely been Brenda's only affair. But the final piece of the puzzle was not yet in place. For all the talk of affairs and leather outfits, of really big hair and "hoochies," the jury had not actually seen physical evidence to support the testimony of sexual promiscuity. The prosecutor thought he had some, though, and he waited until his closing argument to divulge it. This in itself was highly unusual. Evidence cannot magically appear of its own accord at the end of a trial; it must have been previously introduced through a witness. But the prosecution cunningly skirted the rules in the Andrew case. With no fanfare at all, the state had earlier presented suitcases seized from Pavatt and Andrew upon their return from Mexico. It was not until the prosecutor brandished the contents of the suitcases near the end of his final speech—several pairs of thong underwear and lace bras—that the true impact of such evidence was felt:

> This is what we found in [the suitcase]. It's been introduced into evidence. The grieving widow packs this [displaying underwear] to run off with her boyfriend. The grieving widow packs this [displaying another pair] to go sleep in a hotel room with her children and her boyfriend. The grieving widow packs this [again] in her appropriate act of grief.

The spectacle of a prosecutor parading a woman's underwear in front of the jury dumbfounded the defense attorneys, who later claimed they were too shocked to even object. The portrait of Brenda Andrew as an evil woman was complete.

Much of the country has become disenchanted with the death penalty, and executions and death sentences are at national forty-year lows. But Oklahomans still seem partial to the punishment. While Trump won the statewide vote handily in the 2016 election, a ballot question ensuring the constitutionality of the death penalty passed by an even greater margin. Oklahoma ranks first in per capita executions since the reinstatement of capital punishment in 1976, and was the last state to execute a juvenile and an uncontested intellectually disabled person before both actions were declared unconstitutional in the early 2000s. Brenda Andrew would have to navigate this difficult terrain for her appeal.

Her first stop was the Oklahoma Court of Criminal Appeals, where she found a tribunal unbothered by the prosecutor's display of her underwear. Such evidence showed "the extent and the nature of the relationship between Pavatt and [Andrew], and their intentions in fleeing to Mexico—not as a grieving widow, but as a free fugitive living large on a Mexico beach." The court was less cavalier about other evidence, however, finding that a number of mistakes had been made in her trial. Indeed, the court's opinion noted that it was "struggling to find any relevance" to the evidence of her provocative dress, her change of hair color, her coming on to young men at her house. The state fared no better in defending that evidence itself, often veering into the ridiculous, such as its argument that her prior affairs "illustrate [Andrew]'s assertiveness when dealing with, and her ability to manipulate and control, men." Did this sort of evidence have anything to do with a murder trial or a death sentence?

But ridiculous or not, Brenda Andrew was about to learn a hard lesson about legal mistakes, by way of a doctrine that is the bane of appellate lawyers' existence: harmless error. Judges and prosecutors and defense attorneys make mistakes, the doctrine says, but not all mistakes are created equal; and only those mistakes that would have affected the verdict require a new trial. The majority of the Court of Criminal Appeals found that none of the errors would have made the jury vote differently.

The court's opinion was not unanimous, however. Judge Arlene Johnson believed that Andrew should receive a new sentencing. She articulated and condemned the "evil woman" theory at the same time:

> The first stage of this capital murder trial is rife with error. That error, at its most egregious, includes a pattern of introducing evidence that has no purpose other than to hammer home that Brenda Andrew is a bad wife, a bad mother, and a bad woman. The jury was allowed to consider such evidence . . . in violation of the fundamental rule that a defendant must be convicted, if at all, of the crime charged and not of being a bad woman.

While she found the proof of Andrew's guilt too strong to disturb the guilty verdict, she refused to "stretch that rationale far enough to find this jury was unaffected by that evidence in deciding whether this defendant should live or die." Another judge on the court agreed with Johnson and would have gone further, granting Andrew a new trial as well. But those two were not a majority. Brenda Andrew remained on death row.

The next appellate stop was the federal district court of western Oklahoma, a jurisdiction that carried a devastating legacy from the Oklahoma City bombing of 1995. The crime prompted an almost immediate response from the U.S. Congress, and various bills were debated only weeks after the bombing. Civil rights and civil liberties groups spoke eloquently against acting hastily. One speaker begged Congress not to practice the "politics of the last atrocity," a phrase that had originated during the Troubles in Northern Ireland: "Destroying constitutional rights is not the way to build a memorial to the dead in Oklahoma City, nor is it the way to protect Americans from terrorism, nor is it the way to fight terrorism." Others pointed out the country's unfortunate history in the wake of traumatic events—the

Smith Act and its subsequent prosecutions to lock up Communists at the beginning of the Cold War, the internment of Japanese Americans after the attack on Pearl Harbor—and urged caution in the face of a nearly universal demand for action. Such calls went unheeded, however, and almost exactly one year after the bombing the Antiterrorism and Effective Death Penalty Act was signed by President Clinton.

The act, soon to be known as AEDPA and pronounced as "ed-pa," addressed international terrorism, weapons restrictions, criminal alien removal, and various other issues, but its greatest impact by far was on the federal writ of habeas corpus, often called the Great Writ because of its historical role in the protection of individual liberties against government overreach. AEDPA spurred an enduring rash of legal condemnation for its narrowing of the rights of the accused, and more specifically for its requirement that the federal courts defer to state court decisions, even when those courts made clear constitutional errors. It was with this backdrop that Brenda Andrew pursued her federal death penalty appeal, and one of her significant arguments was that the testimony of her sexual history had rendered the trial fundamentally unfair.

Of all the irrelevant evidence of Andrew's promiscuity, perhaps the most extraneous was her affair with a man named Rick Nunley, a sexual relationship that had ended four years before the murder and was labeled "remote" even by the Oklahoma Court of Criminal Appeals. But the court dismissed the importance of the Nunley testimony out of hand:

> Evidence of their sexual affair was limited to one question during his testimony. Thus, even though the evidence of a sexual affair between Nunley and [Andrew] was remote, its significance was a minimal part of the relationship, and the mention of it was harmless in this case.

There was only one problem with the court's analysis—it was wrong. There had been an entire series of questions about their sexual relationship:

Prosecutor: When did you begin to have a more than friendly relationship with the Defendant Brenda Andrew?

A: In the late Fall of '97, probably late October or early November of '97.

Q: Was there something that [sic] particular that caused that relationship to escalate?

A: Brenda seemed to experience common marital problems that I also experienced and we shared those things over the years, that may have contributed to it.

[. . .]

Q: Now, at the time you began your affair with Brenda Andrew were you married, sir?

A: I was married, however, we had filed for divorce I think on October 1 of 1997.

Q: And was Brenda Andrew married?

A: Yes.

Q: Was she married to Rob Andrew?

A: Yes.

Q: Did Rob Andrew know about your relationship with Brenda Andrew at the time it was going on?

A: Not to my knowledge.

Nunley was then questioned about the more relevant insurance policy and the controversy over its ownership. But just in case the earlier point had been missed, the prosecutor returned to the relationship again a few minutes later:

Q. Had your affair ended with Brenda at the time you're testifying about, around the 1st of October of 2001?

A. Yes. We had stopped seeing each other that way for a number of years.

Q. And while you were having an affair with Brenda Andrew was that a sexual relationship?

A. Yes.

And then there was this line of questioning in response to Nunley's testimony that Brenda was "an intelligent person, one that loved her kids dearly, very hospitable hostess, good cook, nice person I thought":

Q: You testified that Brenda Andrew was a very hospitable person. She was really hospitable to you, wasn't she, Mr. Nunley?

A: Yes.

Q: And she was hospitable to Mr. James Higgins as well, wasn't she?

A: I haven't heard his testimony.

Q: She was hospitable to Mr. Pavatt as well, wasn't she?

A: I haven't heard his testimony either.

The Oklahoma court justified the admissibility of the Nunley affair by noting that Brenda shared with him "her hatred for Rob Andrew and her wish that he was dead." This too was incorrect. Indeed, his testimony was quite the opposite:

Q: Were there any discussions with her about how she disliked Rob so much she wanted him dead or anything of that nature?

A: No.

Q: She certainly didn't leave you with any impression . . . that she was going to hurt or harm or kill Rob in any way, did she sir?

A: No, never.

Had the Oklahoma state court actually read the transcript of the trial? If so, they had made some very significant errors. But what consequence did such a casual approach to a judicial opinion have in a federal court?

Much has been written about how the federal courts have been neutered by AEDPA, but even within its restrictive confines the statute makes an exception for what it terms an "unreasonable determination of the facts" by the state court. Since the Oklahoma court had made such clear mistakes in its opinion, how could it possibly have credibly decided whether Brenda Andrew had gotten a fair trial? The task fell to federal Judge Russell, of the Western District of Oklahoma, to sort out fact from fiction.

Russell's opinion did no such sorting, however, and this was very bad news for Brenda Andrew. Quoting the state decision at great length, the judge did not correct a single factual error made by the Oklahoma Court of Criminal Appeals. Referring over and over again to the deference federal courts owe state decisions, and utilizing the double negative that is the hallmark of AEDPA, Russell did not find the Oklahoma court's determination of the facts to be unreasonable. Put in plain English, Andrew had lost every claim.

But her chance of prevailing on appeal was about to take an even worse turn. Ordinarily there is one last stop before you reach the U.S. Supreme Court itself, and that is the federal court of appeals. In Andrew's case she would turn to the Tenth Circuit, but Judge Russell had precluded this appeal by denying something called a Certificate of Appealability—he found that not a single issue in her case was "debatable among jurists of reason." In other words, the judge had determined that her appeal was pointless.

Now what? Andrew had been waiting eleven years for her

number to be called, and her options were rapidly shrinking. What was more, the jangled nerves of Oklahoma's death row had been further shattered by a botched execution that gave pause to even the hardiest capital punishment proponent. After a medical team struggled to get a catheter into one of Clayton Lockett's veins for almost an hour, eyewitnesses watched him writhing and bucking cn the gurney for thirty minutes before the governor called off the execution by telephone from the Oklahoma City Thunder basketball game she had been attending. This did not save Lockett, however; he died of a heart attack while still in the execution chamber ten minutes later.

The ghastly combination of state ineptitude and the inverse of the late Justice Scalia's description of lethal injection as an "enviable . . . quiet death" prompted a lawsuit by a death row inmate named Charles Warner. He had been scheduled for execution the same night as Lockett, but was spared by the governor's phone call, and now he was the lead plaintiff in a legal effort to persuade the state to change its lethal injection protocol. Andrew and nineteen other death row inmates joined the suit, but the litigation did not stop executions in Oklahoma. Warner was put to death in early 2015. His demise, while not as outwardly grotesque as Lockett's, was marred by the state's later concession that it had used the wrong drug in violation of its own protocol. A grand jury investigating the Lockett and Warner debacles described actions by state officials as "negligent," "careless," and "reckless," and the state has not executed anyone since. In the meantime, Oklahoma is exploring the firing squad and nitrogen gas as alternative avenues for capital punishment; and in October 2020 the director of the Oklahoma Department of Corrections announced that it was ready to move forward with the very same drug protocol that had caused the botched executions. No one believes that the results of the investigation will end the death penalty in the state.

A glimmer of hope has crept into the Andrew case, however. A year after Judge Russell found none of her claims worthy of debate, the Tenth Circuit disagreed and granted an appeal on eight different issues. The law is very clear that such a ruling does not herald a winning argument, but at least she now gets to make one. The lead claim charges "that the trial was rendered fundamentally unfair by the admission of irrelevant and salacious facts about Brenda Andrew's sexual appetites and her past adulterous affairs."

It's now been more than three years since her case was argued in the Tenth Circuit, and she is still waiting for the result. To a very real extent, however, her fate has already been determined. As death penalty lawyers have said long before the word came into vogue, she has been "othered"; that is, the prosecution has successfully vilified her character as well as her crime. Deciding whether Brenda Andrew is wretched or evil is not the issue. What we really have to face is our willingness to execute a woman for behavior that has nothing at all to do with criminality.

5

The Lawyer Who Drank
His Client to Death

When people recount their alcohol consumption after a night on the town or even a serious bender, they usually think in terms of drinks or maybe fifths. Very rarely do they calibrate their intake in quarts; most of us would not have a good sense of just how much a quart of vodka actually is. A little more than twenty-one shots, as it turns out. The same amount of alcohol drunk every night by Andy Prince during the death penalty trial of his client, Robert Wayne Holsey.

Of course, that level of inebriation does not occur in isolation—there's collateral damage that always goes with it. And for Andy Prince, the collateral damage was significant. A skilled lawyer who'd gone badly off the rails, Prince had dug a very deep hole for himself by the time of the Holsey trial in February 1997. It's never easy to pinpoint the first sign of a lawyer's money troubles, but Prince was well past the first sign by the time of his appointment to the case in December 1995. A promissory note for $20,000 he'd signed in 1988 had gone bad by June 1995; in August of the same year there were judgments against him from BellSouth and Vanguard Financial totaling $25,000. But the real evidence that he was in the hole for good came shortly after June 1994, when he was hired by Margaret Collins to probate the estate of her common-law husband. At the time the estate stood at $116,000; less than a year later there was no estate at all. As Prince said, he hadn't really considered what he was doing stealing—he'd always intended to pay it back when that one big civil case came along.

His deterioration showed in other ways as well. In June 1996 he had an argument with neighbors at his apartment complex, cursed at them using racial slurs ("[N-word], get the fuck out of my yard or I'll shoot your Black ass"), and threatened them with a gun. He was charged with two counts of pointing a pistol at another, two counts of simple assault, two counts of disorderly conduct, and, of course, public drunkenness.

For Andy Prince, it always came back to alcohol. Even his financial problems were rooted in his drinking—three months before he had written the first of the many checks against the estate that eventually put him in prison, he'd been hit with a complaint from the Athens Regional Medical Center for failure to pay more than $10,000 for a three-week inpatient substance abuse program from 1993. But his drinking had started long before that. By fourteen he already had a problem, and by his late thirties he'd lost his battle with alcoholism countless times. In 1988, with a blood alcohol level almost four times the driving limit and claiming he'd been drunk for two months, he came into the emergency room asking to be detoxified; but as had almost always happened in the past, he signed out against medical advice. In May 1993 he topped that with a near-death .346 blood alcohol level—a few days later, Dr. Thomas Butcher began his psychological evaluation of Prince this way:

When a very intelligent man whose professional life is spent out maneuvering and out smarting other people repetitively makes a serious judgment error based on a belief that has been repeatedly shown to be wrong, he needs to consider that it may be time for him to do some serious revision of his thinking, that is, if he wants to continue to live.

The doctor went on to note that "if he made the kind of mistakes in the courtroom that he makes with his drinking he wouldn't have a professional career to worry about." Three days after the evaluation, Prince checked out of the hospital against medical advice. Not that inpatient treatment was the answer, though. A week after leaving the hospital, he was back and stayed for three weeks; but it didn't take, and two months later he returned to the emergency room with acute intoxication. Yet he was nothing if not resilient. When his treating physician pointed out his family problems (he was struggling through a second marriage), financial difficulties, and legal responsibilities, Andy Prince said he believed he had them "under control." The view from an alcoholic's ledge is likely to be blurry, however. While Prince may have convinced himself that he was under control, events soon proved otherwise.

In the early morning hours of December 17, 1995, Robert Wayne Holsey was arrested for the murder of Deputy Sheriff Will Robinson after fleeing from a robbery of a Jet Food Store in Milledgeville, Georgia, the seat of Baldwin County. The case immediately took on the highest profile—most of the judges from the county went to the deputy's funeral, many sent flowers, and the publicity generated by the killing eventually caused the trial to be moved two counties away. Holsey, like the great majority of those arrested for serious crimes, could not afford to hire a lawyer; he had to depend on a judge to appoint one for him.

Why the court would have chosen Andy Prince for the job

is a mystery. Aside from his long-standing alcohol problem and the financial complaints that were piling up against him, Prince did not generally handle cases in the Milledgeville area. As it turns out, there was no merit selection or careful screening process involved; it doesn't appear to have even been much of a choice. Rather, the selection conjures up the old military trope about volunteering when everyone else takes a step backward. As Prince himself told it: "Because of who the victim was, nobody within the circuit wanted to be appointed to this case. And I told [the judge], sure, I'd take it."

Prince had only one condition—he insisted on picking his co-counsel. He had handled previous capital cases, and with some success, but he had always worked on the more traditional guilt/innocence part of the representation rather than the crucial sentencing aspect of a death penalty case. He asked Rob Westin, a lawyer he'd collaborated with previously; Westin said he'd do it, but almost immediately he was forced to change his mind. Again Prince explained:

> He, Rob contacted me very shortly—and I don't remember the exact time period, but was probably less than a month; it may have been just a week after I had contacted him to see if he would do it and he agreed—and said that he could not be in the Holsey case, that he had gone to the solicitor's office in Baldwin County and had been told that they couldn't believe that he was representing Mr. Holsey and that if he continued to represent him he would never get another deal worked out with that office.

Prince's next attempt to secure co-counsel failed as well, when that lawyer quit after a few months on the case and took a job with the Georgia Attorney General's Office. Finally, only six months before the trial was scheduled to begin, Prince found his "second chair" in Brenda Trammell, a lawyer who practiced in Morgan County, where the Holsey case was to be tried. As she later saw it, she was selected "based on proximity." Here is how she described her role: "I really felt that I was the go-for, waiting for instructions. I had not tried to trial a death penalty case and I waited for him to tell me what to do, and there really was not a lot of direction in that way." According to Prince, "she was about the only one that would take it."

There was still one thing missing. What distinguishes capital murder trials from non-capital ones is the sentencing or penalty phase—if the jury convicts the accused, it then hears more evidence and determines the punishment, usually choosing between life imprisonment without parole and death. A mitigation specialist—referred to by the American Bar Association as "an indispensable member of the defense team throughout all capital proceedings"—gathers information that might save a defendant's life. And indeed a mitigation specialist was ordered for the Holsey case, with funds paid by the court to hire one, but somehow no one knew what had happened to the money, and no mitigation specialist was ever hired. Which may explain Brenda Trammell's answer some years after the Holsey trial:

Q: Was there ever any, when you got into the case, was there any theory with respect to mitigation in the event that he was convicted?
A: No, sir.

But theory or not, Robert Wayne Holsey went on trial for his life in February 1997.

Good capital defense lawyers have the same mantra regardless of where they practice: death is different. By this they mean that the possible state-sanctioned execution of a fellow human being requires extraordinary measures from the defense, and that a capital case must be handled with even greater care than a "regular," or non-capital, murder trial. As the American Bar Association makes clear, "it is universally accepted that the responsibilities of defense counsel in a death penalty case are uniquely demanding."

This is hardly a new concept. More than eighty years ago, in the infamous capital rape case against nine young Black men known as the Scottsboro Boys, the trial judge appointed the entire Scottsboro bar to represent the defendants. The showing of false magnanimity was equivalent to pushing everyone out of a plane with a defective parachute. The U.S. Supreme Court, through Justice Sutherland, rejected this solution, noting that such an arrangement fell far short of the requirement for the appointment of counsel, and that an accused "requires the guiding hand of counsel at every step in the proceedings against him."

But the Holsey defense team did not provide a guiding hand to their client; indeed it appears that the two lawyers were an odd couple, and barely spoke to each other. Andy Prince was a drunk, and Brenda Trammell was a part-time minister who disapproved of alcohol. She recalled stopping by his hotel room once during the trial—he was drinking, and she didn't return again. She also remembered that he called her house one night and was slurring his words; she told him not to call anymore.

Their inability to communicate had a predictable effect on the trial. When it came time for the crucial cross-examination of the state's expert about blood from the victim found on Holsey's shoes, the decision as to who would handle it appears to have been practically a whim, according to Brenda Trammell:

Q: When were you told that you would cross-examine [the state's DNA expert]?

A: Before lunch.

Q: When did she testify?

A: She was testifying. We took a break for us to do the cross, for lunch, and during lunch I had to learn about DNA.

Q: Did you know, had you had any training for DNA before that?

A: No, sir.

Q: Did you know anything about the DNA process?

A: No, sir . . . I was calling during lunch the capital defense people, to ask them what am I supposed to ask about DNA?

Q: And did you learn . . . being thrown into that, that questioning concerning DNA is an extremely technical and complicated area?

A: Definitely.

On February 11, 1997, both sides made their closing arguments and the judge gave final instructions to the jury. At 5:50 that evening, Robert Wayne Holsey was convicted of the armed robbery of the Jet Food Store and the murder of Deputy Sheriff Will Robinson. That was the night Andy Prince called Brenda Trammell for the only time. Drunk. He said he was concerned that the sentencing verdict was not going to be good.

The state presented its case for a death sentence the next morning. Eight witnesses detailed Holsey's criminal background—in addition to the crimes for which he had been convicted, he had pled guilty to an armed robbery with serious bodily injury fourteen years earlier, and two counts of aggravated assault nine years after that. There was a considerable dispute about whether the victims had actually initiated the aggravated assaults, but in the end it hardly mattered—a man was stabbed four times and Holsey pled guilty to it. When the state rested its case, they had painted a stark portrait of a man with a violent past who had killed a deputy sheriff.

The defense did very little to change that portrayal. They called several witnesses to continue the useless debate that Holsey wasn't actually responsible for the aggravated assault cases even though he had pled guilty to them. A few employees from the county jails testified that he hadn't caused any problems while he was in their facilities. Three people from the local Pizza Hut testified that he had been a good employee for six months or so, but that he'd lost the job when he went to jail for the aggravated assaults. The owner of the bar where the assaults had occurred drew some vague conclusions about his mother's neglect of her children and lack of parenting skills. A younger sister of Holsey's begged the jury to let him live, but provided no specifics about her brother or their family. That left only one witness to convey anything of substance about Robert Wayne Holsey. His oldest sister, Regina Holsey.

Regina Holsey was a deputy U.S. marshal. A marine. A veteran of Desert Storm. And a former employee of the same office as victim Will Robinson, the Baldwin County Sheriff's Department. Her direct testimony reads like an underdeveloped roll of film—there are hints of powerful and compelling mitigating evidence on behalf of her brother, but the story never actually gets told. Rather, critical moments are mentioned almost in passing: their father was shot and paralyzed by the police when her mother was pregnant with Wayne (his family called him Wayne, not Robert); he did poorly in school and was considered borderline intellectually disabled; his mother physically beat the children; he was a stutterer and a bed wetter; and his sister Angela and mother, Mary, had mental health problems.

Indeed, it was almost as if Andy Prince felt he was wasting the jury's time. On four separate occasions during the examination of his most critical witness, he noted that the jury could read a document if they wanted to. For instance:

Q: And I'm not, again, just—I'm going to hit a few highlights. This is a juvenile complaint report dated 6-27-65. And I want you to read just the highlighted portion from that second page of that document. And the jury will be able to read it all, but I'm not going to take that much time. I'm going to hit some of the— would you read those highlighted portions, please?

A: The first part says Mr. Courson advised me that Robert was basically a runaway case. He has no supervision at home and refuses to return home. Says Mrs. Holsey would not go to the school, and sent a note with Robert. Robert was not allowed to return. When he tried to come back the principal called the police to remove Robert.

The closing argument, presented by Brenda Trammell, was even more cursory, perhaps because she didn't learn she was going to give it until the night before. In a nine-and-a-half-page speech laden with religious references—the lawyer-minister used the word *God* sixteen times and *Jesus* five—she managed to condense the mitigating evidence for her client into one paragraph:

Not all of us are abused and neglected, cursed at. Not all of us grow up with no father, with no mother in essence who are neglected and are left alone, who are beaten. You know, you have got the records of Angela Holsey. Look at those when you go out. With a foster placement plan that says, "We can't send her back to a parent that won't encourage her in anything; it in actuality encourages her violence." Who is borderline mentally retarded. Wayne is borderline mentally retarded. Does that excuse him? No, there is no excuse. Who stuttered, who wet the bed until he was 12, and no one even takes him to the doctor for it. Who grew up by himself.

She ended with a plea for mercy. But Andy Prince, though drunk, had been correct in his prediction about the sentencing verdict. Less than two hours later the jury rejected mercy, and imposed a sentence of death.

Trouble caught up to Andy Prince shortly after the trial. He removed the final $800 from the estate he'd looted, and took a plea for probation to disorderly conduct for the argument he'd had with his neighbors. Thousands of dollars in judgments piled up against him. And of course the roof caved in soon enough. Eight months after the Holsey trial he surrendered his law license, six months after that he was indicted for theft, and in May 1998 he went to prison for sixteen months. By the time he got around to testifying about his own behavior during the Holsey appeal, he was a freelance paralegal. Here's what he said:

Q: Did you attempt to conceal your difficulty with alcohol from [the trial judge]?
A: I didn't attempt to conceal it, I just didn't parade it around. At the time, I didn't consider I was having any trouble with alcohol.
Q: Why is that?
A: You know, I could drink a quart of alcohol every night and work all day long. I thought I was doing fine.

Q: Since you have become sober, do you have a different opinion now?

A: Absolutely.

Q: And what is your opinion now?

A: Well, what I considered was doing fine at the time was just barely getting by.

Asked if he should have accepted the Holsey appointment in the first place, Prince said, "I shouldn't have been representing anybody in any case." But did it matter that he did?

In the same way that alcoholics see things more clearly when they stop drinking, death penalty cases often come into better focus when good lawyers take over from bad ones. Robert Wayne Holsey's case certainly did. Was it too late? The state of Georgia thought so: maybe Andy Prince was drunk every night, and maybe it would have been better if another attorney had taken the case instead of him, but Robert Wayne Holsey was guilty of murder, and the best lawyers in the country couldn't change that fact. This was nothing more than crying over spilled milk.

But capital cases are more than just questions of guilt or innocence: often the biggest question of all is whether the guilty should live or die. It turned out that a great deal of Holsey's life had not been revealed to the jury. While his below-average intellect and home environment had been touched upon briefly during his sentencing, both took on far greater detail as his appeals unfolded. Holsey had in fact been socially promoted year after year—as early as first grade, he was well behind the other students in basic skills. His math and reading abilities had never gotten past a third-grade level; as a junior high school teacher put it, he "had no smarts and was not playing with a full deck." Two doctors testified that he was not borderline but actually intellectually disabled, which would exempt him from eligibility for the death penalty altogether.

There was much more the jury hadn't heard as well, told by witnesses who would have testified had they only been asked. Wayne's mother, Mary, was legendary in the neighborhood for the fearsome physical abuse she inflicted on her children. If Wayne opened the refrigerator looking for food because he was hungry, he was beaten. If he left their yard, he was beaten. If he wet the bed, which he did until he was a teenager, he was beaten. Curling irons, extension cords, high-heeled shoes, cooking spoons. In the house, on the corner. And there was verbal abuse that went with the beatings: butthole, sissy ass, motherfucker, dumbo, "buck teeth motherfucking monkey." It was all summed up by Sandra Francis, a woman who had grown up with the Holsey children before going off to college and graduate school in New Jersey: "I remember saying prayers of thanks and gratitude to God that I was not one of Mary Holsey's children . . . we called her unit in the projects the Torture Chamber."

At the conclusion of the appellate hearing, a much clearer portrayal of Robert Wayne Holsey had been established: a stuttering, bed-wetting, extremely low-functioning man who had been raised in poverty and terrorized physically and mentally by a vicious, violent, and psychotic mother. The judge hearing the appeal agreed, and wrote that "counsel at trial failed to prepare and present any meaningful mitigation evidence as a defense to the death penalty. In light of this lack of any significant preparation or presentation of such defense, no one can seriously believe that the Petitioner received the constitutional guarantees of the Sixth Amendment right to effective assistance of counsel." Robert Wayne Holsey was going to receive a new sentencing hearing. Or was he? The case headed to the Georgia Supreme Court, which had to answer the same two questions that had just been answered in the court below: Did Andy Prince do a competent job, and would it have mattered if he had?

There is a reason that the "entire Scottsboro bar" did not satisfy the constitutional requirement of counsel when an Alabama trial judge made his outlandish appointment. Fifty years later, the U.S. Supreme Court, in the case of *Strickland v. Washington*, explained why:

> That a person who happens to be a lawyer is present at trial alongside the accused, however, is not enough to satisfy the constitutional command. The Sixth Amendment recognizes the right to the assistance of counsel because it envisions counsel's playing a role that is critical to the ability of the adversarial system to produce just results. An accused is entitled to be assisted by an attorney, whether retained or appointed, who plays the role necessary to ensure that the trial is fair.

In other words, whether it be the entire bar or just one person, whoever represents the accused has a far greater obligation than just standing around with a law license in his pocket. But the Court didn't stop there; if it had, everyone accused of a crime would go looking for the worst attorney he could find as a sort of insurance policy. To prevail on appeal, the condemned also has to show that if his lawyer hadn't done such a poor job, the outcome might reasonably have been different. And there's the rub.

The Georgia Supreme Court opinion in the Holsey case did not mention Andy Prince's alcoholism. Nor his arrests, disbarment, or imprisonment. Instead, the court wrote that it presumed Prince performed deficiently. The opinion didn't actually say that, however. What it said was that Holsey's death sentence was vacated "on the basis of trial counsel's alleged ineffectiveness in preparing and presenting mitigation evidence." That's the word the court used: *alleged*. The opinion actually made it sound as if Prince and Trammell did an outstanding job, describing the evidence found on appeal as "largely cumulative of evidence presented at trial, which highlighted Holsey's limited intelligence, his troubled and abusive home life, his positive contributions at home and elsewhere, and his mother's and sister's mental health issues." The court concluded that the result would not have been different, and reimposed Holsey's death sentence.

How do judges determine whether there is a reasonable probability of a different result? In *Strickland*, the U.S. Supreme Court said that the decision should be objective, assuming that "the decision maker is reasonably, conscientiously, and impartially applying the standards that govern the decision." But is the decision really objective? The death penalty itself is an individual moral choice—and in Georgia, as in most states, if a single juror votes for life a life sentence is imposed. The Georgia Supreme Court was saying that, in their objective opinion, the new evidence would not have changed a single juror's mind. Apparently, that court was not moved by the affidavit of Larry Johnson.

Larry Johnson was a juror in the Holsey trial. He was no stranger to capital cases, and had been a juror in the 1991 case of William Brooks. Brooks had been represented by a team of expert death penalty lawyers led by Stephen Bright, the founder of the Southern Center for Human Rights, and had been given a life sentence in his case. Against the very specific advice of the Georgia Attorney General's Office, which had sent a letter to all of the Holsey jurors advising them that it was in their best interest not to discuss the case with members of Holsey's defense team, Mr. Johnson provided an affidavit about his experience. He found the tone of the government's letter "inappropriate," and said that he knew it was his prerogative to speak to whomever he wanted. Here is what else he said:

> In light of my experience in the *Brooks* case, I was left to assume that Mr. Holsey was one of the "worst of the worst" in our society. I figured that if a deeper or fuller explanation for his violence had been available, surely the lawyers would have presented everything that they could.

And then he reached the rub himself: "Had Mr. Holsey's lawyers provided us jurors with even a small part of the wealth of information concerning . . . his background that I now know is available, it would have made a difference." But whether it would have made a difference to Larry Johnson was of no consequence. To paraphrase George W. Bush, the justices of the Georgia Supreme Court were the deciders, and it had made no difference to them.

Holsey lost again in the federal district court, a consequence of the absurdly named Antiterrorism and Effective Death Penalty Act of 1996, a law designed to limit appeals for death row inmates and compel the federal courts to give great deference to state court decisions. Thus, the only question that remained for the judge hearing Holsey's federal appeal was whether the Georgia Supreme Court had acted unreasonably, and the district court readily concluded it had not. Just as the Georgia court had done, the district judge presumed that Prince had done a deficient job—his drinking, theft, disbarment, and imprisonment was relegated to a footnote in the opinion.

Now he was down to his last appeal, in the Eleventh Circuit Federal Court of Appeals. A three-judge panel heard his case, and all three wrote opinions. Judge Rosemary Barkett argued that the Georgia Supreme Court was indeed unreasonable in its assessment of the facts, going so far as to put that court's use of the word *highlighted* in quotations: "the testimony offered at the sentencing testimony can hardly be characterized as having 'highlighted' Holsey's history of abuse, as the Georgia Supreme Court determined. It hardly comports with the 'Torture Chamber' described by Holsey's neighbors and family members at the [appeals] hearing." She noted that Andy Prince had admitted that he *never* considered putting on evidence of intellectual disability at the trial or the sentencing: "This is not surprising given his own testimony that he was drinking heavily during this time and the malpractice suit and criminal charges concerning his theft of client funds." She compared the Holsey case with the case of Richard Cooper, a shockingly similar capital case wherein three different judges from the Eleventh Circuit granted a new sentencing to Mr. Cooper. Barkett concluded:

> I cannot believe that one juror hearing all of the mitigating evidence would not credit Holsey's experts and lay witnesses and find Holsey to be either fully mentally retarded or borderline mentally retarded and so diminished in his cognitive and behavioral capacity as to be either ineligible for or undeserving of the death penalty. When combined with Holsey's evidence of his horrific child abuse, none of which was presented to his sentencing jury, there is a substantial probability that one juror would not have voted in favor of the death penalty had this evidence been introduced by competent counsel.

Judge Edward Carnes believed the opposite. Indeed, his opinion is practically a reverse image of Judge Barkett's. Using the word *highlighted* without quotations, he compared in great detail the testimony presented at Holsey's sentencing and at his appeals hearing, and wrote:

> To be sure, some of the additional evidence that Holsey's [appeals] counsel presented would have been helpful to Holsey during the sentencing phase of his trial. But at this stage of the case, after the state court has adjudicated his claim on the merits, that helpful evidence is not helpful enough.

Carnes did not dispute the similarity between the Holsey and Cooper cases—rather, he referred to the Cooper case as an "outlier." Whether a judicial outlier or not, the results confirmed the court's decision that effective lawyering would have made a difference in his case. At his new sentencing on March 4, 2014, six jurors voted for a life sentence for Richard Cooper.

The tie was broken by Judge James Edmondson. He agreed with Judge Carnes, and appears to have written his concurrence mostly to complain about the length of his colleague's opinion ("It seems to me that the incidence of long opinions has been on the rise in the last decade, or, at least, more are coming across my desk"). His own opinion, predictably, was brief, and strained to get every last inch from the word *reasonable*:

> Objectively reasonable jurists might disagree about prejudice on this record; but to me, a determination that [Holsey] did not show the required prejudice is within the outside border of the range of reasonable.

Which was how a man going to a death penalty trial with a lawyer who drank a quart of vodka a day and was facing disbarment, assault and theft charges, and eventual imprisonment, found himself inches from execution.

At that point only a few avenues remained for Robert Wayne Holsey. One of them was the counterintuitive question about how the state planned to execute him. Georgia was then enmeshed in a dispute about the drugs it was using for lethal injection, and whether the public was entitled to know how they were made and who was providing them to the state. Georgia was so committed to keeping its execution protocol shrouded in secrecy that it had passed a new law declaring all aspects of lethal injection a "confidential state secret." Less than a year after the law went into effect, the Georgia Supreme Court upheld it, declaring that such secrecy played "a positive role in the functioning of the capital punishment process." Now down to his last hope, Holsey sought clemency from the State Board of Pardons and Paroles.

Clemency, a legal concept hundreds of years old, is most commonly defined as a showing of compassion or forgiveness in judging or punishing. Georgia is one of a handful of states that give this power to a state board rather than a governor: five members are appointed to staggered terms, and a majority is needed to change a death sentence to one of life without parole. Holsey came before them with compelling evidence—a remarkable record of obedience and compliance over the course of his seventeen years on death row, a sincere and consistent commitment to his faith demonstrated by years of service, an incredible letter of support from a man who spent eleven years on the row with him and then was fortunate enough to receive his own clemency. There was the intellectual disability, the deprivation, the violence of the "Torture Chamber." And of course there was the lawyer, the drunken, disbarred, and imprisoned lawyer, given to him by the same state that now wanted to kill him.

It wasn't enough. In language designed to assure the public how seriously it took its task, the Board of Pardons and Paroles released a statement denying clemency, but noting that it had "thoroughly" reviewed all information and documents pertaining to the case, and had "thoroughly" examined the parole case file that included a "comprehensive" history of Robert Holsey's life. The next night, in the execution chamber, Holsey apologized to the victim's family and told his sister he loved her. And then he was gone, and with him the question of what justice he might have received had he been given a lawyer who didn't drink a quart of vodka a night.

6

When a Kid Kills His Longtime
Abuser, Who's the Victim?

You could hardly open a Pennsylvania newspaper in 2012 without running into a story about the prosecution of sexual predators or their enablers. The case of Jerry Sandusky, the Penn State football coach convicted of abusing ten boys, was all over the headlines. Two Philadelphia grand juries, in 2003 and 2011, had documented a massive cover-up of sexual abuse by the Catholic Church that would end up with two priests and a monsignor going to prison—the latter was the first senior church official in the United States convicted of endangering children by covering up abuses by priests under his supervision.

In July 2012, after yet another priest was arrested, District Attorney Seth Williams lauded the alleged victim for speaking out after years of silence: "As we have learned," Williams said, "it is extremely difficult for sexual abuse victims to admit that the assault happened, and then to actually report the abuse to authorities can be even harder for them."

The grand juries had made similar points. The most recent version of Pennsylvania's statutes of limitation, noted the 2003 grand jury report, required prosecutors to initiate sexual abuse cases by the child victim's thirtieth birthday, but "the experts have told us that this statute is still too short. We ourselves have seen that many victims do not come forward until deep into their thirties, forties and even later."

The 2011 grand jury was even more forceful, noting that *most* victims don't come forward "for many years, or even decades." Seven of Sandusky's victims took a combined seventy-three years to report their ordeals. The Pennsylvania legislature responded by passing a law allowing the use of experts at trial to help juries understand how sexual violence affects its victims, and how they typically behave.

But these sex-abuse scandals weren't the only legal dramas capturing the public's attention that year. In September 2012, a man named Terry Williams was in the final throes of an effort to survive a death sentence imposed on him for a crime he'd committed a few months after his eighteenth birthday. The Philadelphia DA's office was working overtime to ensure the commonwealth's first involuntary execution in half a century. But there was something about the DA's enthusiasm that seemed out of place: Terry Williams had been convicted, in separate trials, of murdering two much older men who had sexually abused him as a minor.

In the first case, a jury convicted Williams of third-degree murder after it was made aware of the victim's sexual relationship with his killer. In the second, the jurors never heard evidence of the victim's proclivity for sleeping with teenage boys. They convicted Williams of first-degree murder and sentenced him to die.

After reading a summary of the crime provided by the DA's office, some might conclude that Williams was nothing but a violent psychopath who got what he deserved:

Terrance Williams robbed and murdered two middle-aged gay men. He stabbed Herbert Hamilton more than 20 times and then beat him with a baseball bat. Months later, he lured Amos Norwood to a cemetery where Williams and a friend brutally bludgeoned him to death so they could steal his belongings and take a joy ride to Atlantic City in his car. Williams also committed other robberies, including one in which he broke into the home of an elderly woman on Christmas Eve with a rifle and threatened to blow her "f---ing head off."

But this account leaves out some salient facts: namely, that both men were having sex with Williams, and that Norwood had been doing so since Williams was just thirteen. The robberies the DA describes followed years of sexual victimization. As the Third Circuit Court of Appeals summarized in 2011:

> When Williams was very young, perhaps around the age of six, he was sodomized by a neighbor boy five years his senior. In his early teens, he was repeatedly molested by a teacher. At thirteen, Williams met and began a relationship with Norwood. Norwood was cruel and physically abusive at times; he once allegedly beat Williams with a belt. When Williams was approximately fifteen, he was attacked by an older male while staying in a boys' home. The assailant held a weapon to Williams's neck and forced him to perform fellatio.

The DA's office has contested each of these facts, claiming that "not one of the purported incidents was contemporaneously reported to medical or law enforcement officials." Even after the sexual abuse was revealed a spokesman for the DA characterized the murders as "hate crimes," adding that it was "well past time for some skepticism about [Williams's] self-serving claims, and some sympathy for the trail of victims he has left in his wake."

Yet this view ignored evidence that was present in the district attorney's own files—evidence that was there even before Williams stood trial in 1986. When a condemned person seeks a new sentencing, the appeals court is often confronted with evidence that should have been presented at the original sentencing, but wasn't. The court's task is then to determine whether that evidence would have influenced the outcome. In the months leading up to Williams's execution date, five of the jurors who had condemned him wrote affidavits declaring that they indeed would have voted differently had they known of his sexual relationship with the victim.

In addition, dozens of former prosecutors signed a letter to then governor Tom Corbett, urging him to commute Williams's death sentence, and more than 350,000 people signed an online petition seeking clemency for Williams. After a deputy district attorney suggested in court that Williams's crimes were the result of "gay-prostitute rage," coalitions of sexual-assault survivors from sixteen states signed a letter condemning the Philadelphia district attorney for the "ill-informed stereotypes" his office was perpetuating. "By any definition—legal, ethical, psychological—a sexual encounter between a 13-year-old child and a 51-year-old man is rape," the letter stated. "To call this 'prostitution' and imply agency and willing participation on the part of a 13-year-old boy is unacceptable." But none of those things persuaded a court to grant Williams a new sentencing hearing.

A few weeks before the execution date, Shawn Nolan, one of Williams's federal defenders, appeared at a clemency hearing before the Pennsylvania Board of Pardons. Yes, Williams had lost all of his appeals, Nolan acknowledged, but "is that a reason to kill this battered, sexually abused, barely 18-year-old kid?" Just the previous week, he reminded the board, one of the prosecutors had been asked, "Why are you fighting so hard to execute this man? After 50 years of no executions like that, why this man?"

Pennsylvania's attorney general, one of the presiding board members, asked whether Nolan was "seriously contending" that the DA's office was "pursuing this merely because they won the case?"

"Yes," Nolan replied. Minutes later, as if to confirm what Nolan had just said, an assistant district attorney told the board that it was "no secret that the reason we're here today, and the reasons these proceedings are unfamiliar, is that this is the only contested Pennsylvania death penalty case that has not been reversed by either state or federal court in many years." Indeed, hundreds of death sentences had been overturned for reasons ranging from the hiding of evidence to the illegal disqualification of Black jurors to just plain incompetent lawyering. But this case had survived the scrutiny of the courts.

As the day approached, the signatures on the clemency petition continued to pile up, as did the mail. Letters poured into the governor's office from retired judges and child advocates, law professors, mental health professionals, and clergy. Editorials against the execution appeared in newspapers across the state. Even the victim's widow wrote a letter stating that she had forgiven Williams and did not want to see his sentence carried out. Yet the prosecution pushed on, leaving the question raised at the clemency hearing still hanging. Was it possible that Philadelphia's district attorney wanted to execute Terry Williams simply because he could?

Most crime stories are best told chronologically. But the pivotal moment in the Terry Williams legal saga came twenty-eight years after the crime, just days before his scheduled execution. The setting: the courtroom of Judge Teresa Sarmina, a former prosecutor assigned to oversee last-minute appeals in the case. Sarmina (who by coincidence had presided over the landmark Catholic Church sex-abuse trial only months before) took what she deemed "extraordinary measures" to vet the fairness of Williams's death verdict. She ordered Andrea Foulkes—Williams's prosecutor, by then a lawyer with the U.S. Attorney's Office in Philadelphia—to testify about her handling of Williams's two trials. Sarmina also ordered the police department's homicide files and the district attorney's trial files brought to her courtroom for examination. She wanted to be confident, she said, that the verdict "was what the word 'verdict' means: To speak the truth."

The search for the truth in a criminal case always begins with the prosecution. A homicide trial in particular takes shape in the district attorney's office long before a jury is selected—and sometimes before a suspect is even arrested. Investigations are launched, statements taken, reports completed, and by law, any information that might conceivably be helpful to the accused must be shared with the defense. This is a constitutional obligation, and yet the law books are replete with cases in which such exculpatory evidence is never passed along.

Judge Sarmina wrote in the *Williams* case that the paperwork involving victim Amos Norwood had been "sanitized." This was a polite way of putting it. The prosecution had omitted portions of two witness statements before turning them over, thereby eliminating the evidence of Norwood's sexual proclivities. Although the most sordid details weren't revealed at the time, Norwood, fifty-six, was known to have engaged in very suspicious behavior with young boys. Before it was redacted by the prosecutors, one police report had indicated that Norwood disappeared overnight with a teenage boy and, upon returning home the next day, told his wife he'd been kidnapped. The other censored document recounted that a mother from Norwood's church had complained of his sexual advances toward her underage son.

Prosecutor Foulkes's handwritten notes—which were also withheld from the defense and made a cryptic and disparaging reference to a presumed police "continued invest. for 'faggot squad'"—indicated that she was aware of the victim's appetites. Foulkes later conceded to Sarmina that she suspected a "sexual connection" between Williams and Norwood: "Of course it occurred to me." But she didn't share this with the defense.

To understand why, it's necessary to look at the first murder Williams committed, when he was seventeen. The victim was fifty-one-year-old Herbert Hamilton, who had a history of paying for sex with teenage boys. Hamilton had been in such a relationship with Williams, who ultimately beat and stabbed him repeatedly before dousing his body with kerosene in a failed attempt to dispose of it—"I loved you" was scrawled in toothpaste on Hamilton's bathroom mirror. After hearing the evidence, the jury acquitted Williams of first-degree murder and instead found him guilty of third-degree murder, which carried a far lesser penalty.

Foulkes had sought death in that case, too, but she professed to have been satisfied with the outcome: "I didn't care what the verdict was as long as the jury considered all the evidence," she later testified. Judge Sarmina didn't believe her: "The third degree verdict in the Hamilton case," she wrote, "colored Ms. Foulkes' decisions when she prosecuted [Williams] for the murder of Amos Norwood." Indeed, less than a year after the Hamilton trial, Foulkes told the Norwood jury that Williams had killed him "for no other reason but that a kind man offered him a ride home . . . He has taken two lives, two innocent lives of persons who were older and perhaps unable certainly to defend themselves against the violence that he inflicted upon them. He thought of no one but himself, and he had no reason to commit these crimes." That jury, none the wiser, sentenced Williams to death.

Sarmina ultimately stayed Williams's execution and granted him a new sentencing hearing, at which a jury would be able to hear the suppressed evidence. But far from being chastened, the Philadelphia DA's office dug in its heels. There were other courts to turn to. Higher courts.

The Supreme Court of Pennsylvania was no friend to capital defendants. In the five years before the *Williams* case came onto its docket, the court, led by Chief Justice Ronald Castille, had ruled in favor of the death penalty 90 percent of the time. This wasn't too surprising, given that Castille had been elected to his judgeship in 1993 as the law-and-order alternative to a candidate he labeled soft on crime. (He became chief justice in 2008.) Before joining the court, he had been Philadelphia's district attorney.

"Castille and his prosecutors sent 45 people to death row during their tenure, accounting for more than a quarter of the state's death row population," the *Pittsburgh Post-Gazette* noted in 1993. "Castille wears the statistic as a badge. And he is running for the high court as if it were exclusively the state's chief criminal court rather than a forum for a broad range of legal issues." Castille was pretty clear about where he stood: "You ask people to vote for you, they want to know where you stand on the death penalty," he told the *Legal Intelligencer*, a law journal. "I can certainly say I sent 45 people to death row as District Attorney of Philadelphia. They sort of get the hint."

One of the forty-five was Terry Williams. In fact, it was Castille who, in a handwritten note to the chief of his homicide unit, had approved Williams's capital prosecution in 1986. You could make a strong argument that a judge in his position should recuse himself from the appeals process, but Castille had a fraught relationship with the Federal Community Defender Office, a group of lawyers who represent numerous death row inmates, including Williams. Castille claimed that federal lawyers had no business appearing in state courts. He complained bitterly over the years about their "prolix and abusive pleadings" and about all the resources they dedicated to defending death row inmates—"something one would expect in major litigation involving large law firms."

The defenders, for their part, routinely filed motions arguing that Castille had no business ruling on the appeals of prisoners whose prosecutions he had approved—particularly not in a case in which his office was found to have suppressed evidence helpful to the defense. But as chief justice, Castille had the last word. He denied all such motions, and accused the federal defenders of writing "scurrilously," making "scandalous misrepresentations," and having a "perverse worldview."

Thus it stood on October 1, 2012, when Williams's attorneys filed a motion asking Castille to recuse himself from their client's appeal. The chief justice denied it that very day, along with a second request—to let the full Pennsylvania Supreme Court rule on the appropriateness of his involvement.

You might assume that a prosecutor who hides key evidence, especially in a death penalty case, would be subject to discipline—if not criminal charges. But courts are as loath to punish a prosecutor as they are to assist a murderer. The Pennsylvania Supreme Court's ruling in *Commonwealth v. Terrance Williams*, which was released in December 2014, contained not so much as a footnote scolding Foulkes for what Judge Sarmina politely termed "gamesmanship." Instead, the court excoriated Williams for failing to make an issue of his sexual abuse at the hands of the older man. These were, in fact, the prosecution's own arguments, coming from the same DA's office that had recently acknowledged how excruciatingly difficult it was for sexual abuse victims to go public. Of Williams, the court wrote:

> He could have argued Norwood's homosexual proclivities developed into sexual abuse, leading to rage and ultimate murder of Norwood . . . However, [Williams] chose not to do so. Instead, [he] perjured himself at trial, testifying he did not know the victim, had never seen him before, took no part in the murder, and had no reason to be angry with him or wish to harm him.

Castille, who was on his way out due to a mandatory age retirement, voted with the majority but couldn't resist taking a final salvo at the federal defenders' "blatantly frivolous" litigation. In a concurring opinion, he warned the lower courts not to let themselves be turned into circuses with the defenders as "ringmasters." And he upbraided Sarmina for letting Williams's lawyers scour the government's files. The information they revealed, he wrote, had smeared Norwood's character.

The Pennsylvania Supreme Court reinstated Williams's death sentence and ordered the court record sent to the outgoing governor Corbett, who just before leaving office set the execution date for March 4, 2015. Following it through would fall to his successor, Governor Tom Wolf.

To understand why Williams might have denied knowing Norwood, it helps to go back to the first day of jury selection in his capital trial, when Williams announced to the court that he'd only met his lawyer the day before and he wanted a new one. The defense lawyer, assigned to Williams's case by the Philadelphia court system, acknowledged that this was true. Williams, he explained, was incarcerated in a prison far from the city, so he'd relied on his associate for "a lot of the detail work." When the judge asked which prison Williams was housed in, the lawyer had to turn to his client to ask where he'd been held. The judge nevertheless deemed the attorney "very adequate" and denied Williams's request for a replacement. Whether or not the attorney's preparation was truly adequate—a federal judge would later deem his performance "constitutionally deficient"—one thing was clear: there was no trust between the client and his lawyer. Did the prosecutors truly expect an eighteen-year-old facing a possible death sentence to have a frank discussion about his sexual victimization with a court-appointed lawyer he'd just met?

As the first Pennsylvania execution of the twenty-first century loomed, Governor Wolf made a historic announcement: he was granting a reprieve to Terry Williams and any other inmate facing execution until a state task force completed a study of the death penalty and officials had a chance to act on its recommendations. In a five-page memo, Wolf listed race discrimination, bad lawyering, high costs, and the threat of executing an innocent man among the reasons for his decision.

The announcement was no great surprise, given that Wolf and all of his Democratic primary rivals supported putting a moratorium on executions—and that Wolf had handily defeated a pro–death penalty incumbent in the general election. Even the new chief justice of the Pennsylvania Supreme Court had declared the system in "disrepair," and had written extensively on its failings. But death penalty supporters were furious. Seth Williams was among the first to lash out. The people who would be the "most grateful," the district attorney announced, "are the guiltiest, cruelest, most vicious killers on death row." As for Terry Williams, the DA was "weary of this murderer's effort to portray himself as a victim." He failed to mention, of course, the censored police reports, or the Board of Pardons'

3–2 vote in Williams's favor (a unanimous vote is required for clemency). He simply reiterated that the prisoner was guilty of heinous crimes. "The governor's action today was an injustice to the citizens of this state," the DA concluded. "And to victims of crime."

Several weeks later, during a televised debate, Seth Williams further articulated his case: Terry Williams, he said, "brutally beat to death two gay men because he was extorting them." This was a bewildering claim from the head of an office that prosecuted hundreds of sexual abuse cases a year: you could spend decades digging through the Philadelphia court dockets and be hard pressed to find a case in which teenage boys hired to service middle-aged men were charged with extortion.

But the district attorney didn't stop there. Explaining that he agreed the death penalty was appropriate only in the "worst of the worst of the worst" cases, he attempted to describe how the systemic problems the governor had described did not apply to Williams: "Every appellate court has said issues of racism, yes, they exist in the criminal justice system, but not in this case. Cases of people not being given the attorneys that are appropriate, that exists, but not in this case . . ."

Each of these statements had at best a casual relationship to the truth. Take the race issue. About a month before jury selection commenced in the Norwood case, the U.S. Supreme Court heard arguments in *Batson v. Kentucky*, a case that led to the ban on lawyers disqualifying people from the jury pool on account of their race. Indeed, fourteen of the sixteen jurors disqualified by Williams's prosecutor were Black—even though African Americans made up less than half of the jury pool. A federal judge later found that these numbers suggested discrimination, but he accepted prosecutor Foulkes's "race-neutral" reasons for eliminating the jurors, and concluded that there had been no constitutional violation. (This was five years before Judge Sarmina determined that the prosecution with-held key evidence.)

The district attorney's claim that Terry Williams received appropriate counsel was even more incredible. Had he forgotten that Williams's court-appointed attorney didn't even bother to meet with his client until the day before the trial? Or the court finding that the lawyer's performance was "constitutionally deficient"? (He would later have his law license suspended for his role in a wire-fraud scheme, according to court documents; the associate who did the "detail work" was disbarred for other reasons.) Was this really the quality of lawyering appropriate for a man whose life was at stake?

Seth Williams was hardly the only elected official grand-standing over the reprieve. State Representative Mike Vereb introduced a House resolution asking the governor to reverse his action, and he accused Wolf of "standing with some of the worst criminals in Pennsylvania and against their victims." Mamie Norwood, the victim's spouse, responded with an open letter to Vereb and DA Williams:

> I read your resolution which says that Governor Wolf has caused me and my family unnecessary heartache by stop-ping Terry Williams's execution and I am shocked and upset that you and other politicians are using me and saying things that are not true. You are the ones now causing me unnecessary heartache . . . I am asking that you please stop trying to execute Terry Williams. And please don't use me for your own political gain or to get your name in the news. You should be truly ashamed of yourselves.

Twelve days later, Amos Norwood's daughter provided a state-ment supporting an end to the death penalty, but calling for the execution of the man who murdered her father. Terry Williams had become a political football.

Before the ink was dry on the reprieve, District Attorney Williams moved to challenge it in court. In September 2015, the Pennsylvania Supreme Court heard arguments on whether the governor had acted legally under the state constitution. Pennsylvania governors had been granting reprieves for hundreds of years and no court had ever struck one down. What was in dispute, from the DA's perspective, was Wolf's power to impose a moratorium, and his rationale for doing so—namely that the system of capital punishment was "riddled with flaws, making it error-prone, expensive, and anything but infallible."

The Pennsylvania court wasn't keen on analyzing the governor's conclusions. "You're asking us to overturn [his] political pronouncement," one of the justices told the chief of the district attorney's appeals unit. "He could easily have [granted the reprieve] without announcing it as some kind of policy." The argument barely mentioned Terry Williams, and when the new chief justice urged Williams's lawyer to "focus on the interest of your client," the response was painfully obvious: "Mr. Williams has a strong interest. Indeed, his life depends on the court respecting the governor's constitutional reprieve power."

But the Williams case was about to take on significance well beyond the commonwealth. As the Pennsylvania Supreme Court pondered the governor's ability to grant a reprieve, the U.S. Supreme Court announced that it would consider the propriety of former chief justice Castille's participation in the case. Castille had personally authorized Williams's capital prosecution, campaigned for the state supreme court as a death penalty supporter, and voted to deny Williams's appeal after the office he'd formerly run had been caught hiding evidence. It was hard to imagine a more compelling case for a judge to recuse himself, and in fact that was exactly what the highest court found:

> Chief Justice Castille's significant, personal involvement in a critical decision in Williams's case gave rise to an unacceptable risk of actual bias. This risk so endangered the appearance of neutrality that his participation in the case must be forbidden if the guarantee of due process is to be adequately implemented.

While Castille was being reprimanded, the Philadelphia district attorney continued to attack the governor's "flagrantly unconstitutional" reprieve. But things were about to take a turn for the worse in Seth Williams's life as well. In March 2017, he was indicted for bribery, extortion, and other fraud charges, ultimately landing him in a federal prison for a five-year sentence. In October 2017 he agreed to his own disbarment; and after serving three years, he was released from custody.

And what of Andrea Foulkes, who had prosecuted both of Williams's cases when he was a teenager? Long gone from the Philadelphia District Attorney's Office when Sarmina had accused her of improperly withholding evidence in 2012, her employer at the time immediately came to her defense, declaring that she was "an outstanding prosecutor with an impeccable record for integrity, professionalism, and dedication to public service." That employer was the U.S. Attorney's Office for the Eastern District of Pennsylvania, where she is still working nine years later.

And finally, what of Terry Williams? By August 2017, when his case returned to the Pennsylvania Supreme Court, the personnel on the court had changed, and Williams was given a new penalty phase. The new district attorney in Philadelphia,

Larry Krasner, had won a convincing victory to replace his disgraced predecessor, running on a progressive criminal justice platform that included ending the death penalty in a city that had long promoted its use. Krasner's office decided not to seek another death sentence, and Williams moved from death row to general population.

In 2019, a new development surfaced in his other murder case, causing it to unravel in much the same way as the case that had sent him to death row. Judge Sarmina ordered the prosecution to reveal the contents of its file, and to the surprise of practically no one the defense found exculpatory evidence in that file as well. Williams had always claimed that he'd killed Herbert Hamilton in self-defense, after the older man had tried to force him to pose naked and then stabbed him in the face. His defense attorney even possessed a medical record indicating a slashing to the face, but the record had no identifying information on it, and Foulkes refused to agree that it was Williams who had suffered the injury, going so far as to argue to the judge that he "was making this story up." Turned out he wasn't, though: when the prosecution file was opened to the defense decades later, the medical record was right there, and with all the biographical information to indicate that it was Williams's. Krasner's office dismissed the case entirely in 2020.

Terry Williams, the subject of a U.S. Supreme Court opinion, a moratorium on executions, and a near victim of one himself, is now safe from capital punishment and forging ahead with his appeals in the Norwood case. Nine years have passed, and he continues to search for an honest answer to the question his lawyers first raised at his clemency hearing, when he was hours from death: Why him?

7

The Confessions of Innocent Men

Any good criminal defense attorney will tell you to say four words if you are about to be arrested for murder: *I want a law-yer*. This is simple advice and should be easy to remember during an interrogation, but not everyone recalls it under ac-cusative pressure. Some people make matters worse for them-selves in the face of strong evidence. Others provide an alibi or identify another person as the perpetrator. Many succumb to the wiles of homicide detectives and implicate themselves to some lesser degree in the crime, heeding the admonition that a partial loss is better than going down for the whole thing. Some accused people are tricked into confessing, and some confess to crimes they did not commit. A certain percentage, worn down by conscience or questioning or the simple desire to get the interrogation over with, provide a detailed and honest explanation for what they did.

And then there's Anthony Sylvanus. He came to the atten-tion of Philadelphia homicide detectives in March 2001 while minding his own business at the State Correctional Institution at Albion—a stone's throw from Lake Erie, and as far away from his crime as the geography of Pennsylvania allows—where he was serving a sentence of ten to twenty years. While some-one doing that much time can't be said to have much luck, whatever small amount he did possess was about to run out. Two events would cause this turn: the advent of the automated fingerprint identification system, and a random conversation between a police captain in Philadelphia and a murder victim's granddaughter.

The automated fingerprint identification system is an algorithm-driven method of comparing millions of known fin-gerprints to a single partial print. The process replaced the labor-intensive manual examinations required since police had begun using fingerprint identification in the late nineteenth century. The Philadelphia Police Department started employ-ing the computer technology in the early 1990s and by 2000 could, without much trouble at all, plug in a print and see who came out. That was the year Ann Ruane's granddaughter, at-tending a piano lesson for her daughter, asked a fellow parent, Philadelphia Police Captain Alan Kurtz, if he might look into her grandmother's unsolved murder from 1980.

The phrase *cold case* has now entered the lexicon. DNA breakthroughs and internet databases have made prosecutions and exonerations for old crimes more common today, and var-ious television shows feature law enforcement units dedicated solely to righting a wrong, no matter how frozen in time that wrong might be. Such units were less well known in 2000, and had Kurtz not been asked to look into the twenty-year-old crime, Ann Ruane's murder might have remained unsolved. But a fingerprint happened to have survived from the case, and that print led to Anthony Sylvanus.

Not long after the print was identified, Sylvanus was trans-ported across the diagonal of the state and confronted by Phil-adelphia homicide detectives. His initial denial of the crime was perfunctory, and after being told of the fingerprint hit, he quickly confessed to pushing his way into Ann Ruane's house, beating her to death, and ransacking her home for drug money. The Defender Association of Philadelphia was appointed to represent him, and the crime, although old, appeared headed toward a routine and typical prosecution. Given his full confession, the case seemed certain to end in conviction. Less obvious at the time was the strange path the case would take from there.

As for Sylvanus, he was no novice to the criminal justice system—surely he realized that his confession had sealed his doom. Perhaps this realization is what motivated him to do what he did next, or maybe his conscience simply caught up with him. Whatever the reason, he decided that he had more to say. Much more. While his lawyers begged him to stop talking, and peppered the homicide unit and the district attorney's office with letters and faxes admonishing them to cease their interrogations, Sylvanus defiantly insisted that he knew and understood his rights and wanted to share more about other killings. This offer obviously pleased the prosecutors, who informed the Defender Association that they would not seek the death penalty against Sylvanus; they simply wanted to know everything he knew. When all was said and done, Anthony Sylvanus confessed to five murders—all senior citizens, all to get money for drugs, and all between May 1980 and January 1981. He was immediately charged with four of the murders, but a problem arose with the fifth. Two other men seemed to be serving time for that one. Long time.

The last murder Anthony Sylvanus confessed to was Dr. Charles Langley's beating, strangulation, and robbery. Langley, age sixty-three, was an optometrist in the Kensington area of Philadelphia, a run-down neighborhood of crumbling storefronts in the shadow of the El. On the afternoon of January 15, 1981, the police found him in his office, choked by his own necktie; $123 and a wristwatch had been taken. Detective Frank Suminski was assigned to the case, and the murder left him with one clue: whoever had killed Langley had used his hand to "chop" him in the back of his neck.

The detective scoured the local hospitals, and soon learned that a man named Russell had been admitted to Episcopal Hospital with an injured hand the evening of the crime. Maybe it wasn't the best lead Suminski had ever had, but it was a start. The man had given the hospital a fake last name and address, but three weeks later, Russell Weinberger was escorted into police headquarters, where he told Suminski that he had broken his pinky finger helping move a refrigerator.

The detective elicited some testimony from Weinberger that surely gave him pause. Although Weinberger said he had injured his hand before the murder took place, he also said he did not go to the hospital until afterward, because he "was pretty well drunk." Though twenty-five days had passed since the crime, Weinberger, when told of the murder, said he knew exactly where he had been—at home—when it was committed. But his recounting of the accident that injured his hand was not consistent. At one point, he said he had been at Front and Cumberland Streets when the refrigerator dropped. Later, he said he'd been at 2507 Kensington Avenue, only a few dozen yards from Langley's office. Still, Weinberger denied ever having seen the eye doctor or having been in his office, and identified the man who dropped the refrigerator that broke his finger as "Oscar." Weinberger said he knew Oscar from "drinking with us," and named other fellow drinkers as "Alvin" and "Felix." Asked who he thought might have committed the murder, Weinberger said Alvin and Felix because "they both like to beat up on old men." After Weinberger gave his statement, the police administered a lie-detector test, during which he again denied knowing anything about the murder. The results were "inconclusive."

You might wonder why a lie-detector test would be given at all, since the results have never been proven reliable and thus are not admissible in court. The answer depends on who you ask. Many police detectives will tell you that the examination actually works, and helps them know if they're on the right track. Defense attorneys will say that taking the test, and then being told anything other than "you've passed with flying colors," is inherently coercive. Regardless of perspective, a finding of "inconclusive" was not likely to end the matter.

Little question exists that Suminski liked Weinberger for the murder. The next day, the police went to the Kensington neighborhood and picked up Alvin Papas, which prompted Oscar Vasquez to go see the homicide detectives himself and deny whatever Papas had told them. At that point, though, the investigation looked like a bad case of Whisper Down the Lane. Papas said nothing about falling refrigerators, and had not even been asked about one; but Vasquez told a detective that Papas had accused him of delivering a refrigerator to Langley's office, and that this was untrue. A man named James Ferrares, who accompanied Vasquez to the police station, denied that the imaginary refrigerator in the doctor's office had come from his store. The investigation appeared to be going nowhere.

But one seemingly useful opinion emerged: that the third man Weinberger had identified, Felix Rodriguez, was not a nice guy, especially when he was drinking. Papas said that Rodriguez was a troublemaker, and that he was capable of killing, particularly when he was "boozed up." Furthermore, according to Papas, Rodriguez had disappeared from the neighborhood after the eye doctor's murder and had just started reappearing again.

Tracking down Felix Rodriguez took more than a month. Suminski eventually found him standing on the sidewalk before a junk shop a few blocks from the crime scene. According to the detective, Rodriguez came along willingly, and even sat in the back of an unlocked police car while Suminski went to two hardware stores, doing some personal shopping. When they finally arrived at the homicide unit, the detective put some papers together to prepare for an interview, leaving Rodriguez alone in a room for half an hour. Nothing of consequence had occurred between the two men.

Which made the following exchange between the prosecutor and the detective at Felix Rodriguez's eventual murder trial all the more shocking:

Q: What happened when you came back in to speak to Mister Rodriguez?

A: He admitted killing the doctor and said he wanted to tell the truth.

Q: Had you asked him any questions at that point?

A: No. As a matter of fact I was quite shocked at that.

Q: Had you warned him of his constitutional rights?

A: At that time, no. No.

Q: As best you can remember, what were the words that Mister Rodriguez said when you walked back into the room?

A: He said, I want to tell the truth. I killed him. I want to tell the truth.

Q: And what did you say as soon as he said those words?

A: I said, don't say anything else until I read you your rights. I don't want to hear another thing.

Out of the blue, and with no evidence against him, Felix Rodriguez had confessed to Dr. Charles Langley's murder.

People have been admitting to things they haven't done for as long as they've been committing crimes. On the North American continent, prominent examples reach back to 1692 and the Salem witch trials. DNA exonerations over the past twenty-four years have established not only how error-prone our system of justice is, but how more than a quarter of those wrongly convicted have been inculpated by their own words. Now an entire body of scientific research is devoted to the phenomenon of the false confession. In his article "The Psychology of Confessions," Saul Kassin, a professor of psychology at the John Jay College of Criminal Justice, details three different categories of false confession: voluntary, compliant, and internalized.

Voluntary false confessions are the best known, the most easily disproved, and perhaps the simplest to understand. They are prompted not by police behavior but rather by a need for attention or self-punishment. For obvious reasons, these confessions contain only facts known to the public; they surface in high-profile cases. The kidnapping of Charles Lindbergh's twenty-month-old baby, labeled the "crime of the century" due to Lindbergh's celebrity for his solo flight across the Atlantic, garnered hundreds of such confessions.

Compliant false confessions are the opposite of voluntary confessions. They are coerced by police conduct, and are generally made in the hope of ending the coercion. What stressors would make someone confess to a horrible crime, knowing that the confession's long-term implications would far outweigh any short-term relief? Torture, of course: physical violence, or the threat of future violence such as execution or prison rape. But the coercion need not be nearly as severe as that. Promises of food, a phone call, drugs to feed a habit—all of these have led to compliant false confessions. The guarantee of sleep or simply being left alone has been enough to get an innocent person to admit to a horrendous crime. Even the illogical promise to get to go home was sufficient to get five innocent New York City teenagers to confess, completely independently, to a Central Park jogger's rape.

Internalized false confessions differ from voluntary and compliant ones in a significant way: the confessor comes to believe that he may be guilty of the crime. Richard Leo, a law professor at the University of San Francisco, prefers to call them *persuaded* rather than *internalized*, and explains that such confessions result from interrogations that "shatter the confidence you have in the reliability of your own memory." In essence, some people begin to doubt their own memories, and start to instead believe that they might have done something awful, sometimes confabulating false memories in the process.

Even when they are false, confessions are incredibly powerful. Academics studying the importance of confessions in criminal trials have come to a perhaps unsurprising conclusion: other than physical evidence such as DNA or fingerprints left at the scene of a crime—and in some documented cases even in spite of exculpatory DNA or other physical evidence—a confession is the most powerful proof of guilt. But confessions are not nearly as reliable as DNA.

Multiple recent studies have shown that jurors approach confessions counterintuitively. In surveys, people seem to understand that confessions are occasionally false—previous confessors' high-profile DNA exonerations allow no other conclusion. Jurors also understand that police interrogations are designed to break down a person's will to deny culpability. But those same survey respondents, by a large percentage, do not think that they would ever succumb to such an interrogation; and they can't accept the possibility that the man in the dock might have admitted to a horrible crime he did not commit, particularly when the risk of doing so might be a death sentence.

"Mock jurors have told us time and time again that they recognize the power of psychological coercion, and that it might lead an innocent person to falsely confess," says Leo, who has studied the science of confessions for two decades. "But those same jurors also see such behavior as self-destructive rather than involuntary, and they believe that they would be able to withstand the coercive techniques utilized by the police." What this thinking leads to, says Leo, is an overwhelming tendency to accept confessions at face value.

So many years later, determining how the Rodriguez jury received the testimony of Detective Suminski is impossible. Did it seem strange to them that a man might blurt out a confession to murder for no reason other than being left alone in a room for thirty minutes? Or did they believe that the detective had used skillful interrogation to extract the truth? Suminski himself testified as if no interrogation had taken place at all. After pausing his conversation with Rodriguez to give him his *Miranda* warnings, Suminski began taking a written statement from the now-confessed murderer. Yet the written confession bears little similarity to the oral admission Suminski claimed to have heard—almost as if Rodriguez forgot what he'd said only a few minutes earlier. When asked what happened on the day of the murder, he began talking about a refrigerator delivery. Vasquez and Weinberger, he said, had helped him take the appliance, not to the doctor's office or to Front and Cumberland Streets, but to a house blocks away on Green Street; then Rodriguez and Weinberger went out and bought two bottles of Thunderbird. They drank the wine on some school steps just down the block from the doctor's office, saw police cars arrive at the crime scene, and watched officers remove Charles Langley's body.

"Then I told Russell I'm going to go around Front Street, because I don't want anyone to mess with me," Rodriguez told the detective.

"Why didn't you want anyone to mess with you?" Suminski asked, according to the written confession.

"I don't want to go to jail."

"Why would you worry about going to jail, if you didn't do anything?"

"The people in that neighborhood always bother you and say things."

In short, Felix Rodriguez wasn't confessing at all.

But midway through the interrogation, things took an inexplicable turn, prompted by this innocuous question: "Felix, is there anything else you want to tell me?" Suddenly, there was. Rodriguez said he wanted to tell the truth, then went on to detail how he had murdered Langley, with Russell Weinberger's help. Weinberger, according to Rodriguez, suggested the doctor's office as a likely spot for them to get money, and Rodriguez hit the doctor in the face with a stick while Weinberger choked him. At this point, the detective noted that Rodriguez started crying and said, "I only wanted to get some money. I didn't mean to kill him!" A little later, Suminski asked Rodriguez whether Weinberger had hurt his hand. "Yes, his right hand, when he was punching Doctor." Then Rodriguez identified Weinberger in Philadelphia police photo No. 559645.

Detectives often have a suspect review his written statement and add his initials to any mistakes that might have been made during the transcription. Indeed, experienced detectives often make small mistakes on purpose, so that the accused can initial them to indicate that he read the statement over carefully. Although many corrections and parenthetical additions were made to the Felix Rodriguez statement, no initials appear at all. However, his signature and the date of the statement appear clearly at the bottom of all six pages. Thus, while no evidence supports the fact that Rodriguez carefully read over the confession, more than enough shows that he saw each page. The investigation was starting to come together after all.

One other loose end remained: Russell Weinberger. More than a month earlier, he had denied everything, but three days after the Rodriguez confession, he told a very different story to Detective Suminski. In most ways, Weinberger's new version was similar to what Rodriguez had said: both men had been drinking Thunderbird; both had a hand in beating the doctor; they split the take. Whereas Rodriguez said the robbery had been Weinberger's idea, Weinberger blamed Rodriguez—not an unusual state of affairs when men turn on each other—but for the most part, the statements fit neatly together. Again, as with Rodriguez's statement, no initialed corrections appeared on Weinberger's statement, but Weinberger's signature—an extraordinarily neat and childlike autograph—appeared on every page. Toward the statement's end, Weinberger drew a map to show where they had taken the doctor's watch to sell it: to Cumberland Street, two blocks from Weinberger's house. He spelled the street name "Cumlbirlin."

No lie-detector test was administered this time around. As far as the Commonwealth of Pennsylvania was concerned, the investigation of Dr. Langley's killing was closed.

The case against Felix Rodriguez and Russell Weinberger did not immediately proceed to trial. First some legal wrangling took place—a judge in the Court of Common Pleas of Philadelphia ruled that Rodriguez's statement was inadmissible, then the Superior Court of Pennsylvania reversed that ruling. By the time the parties were finally ready to go to trial, four and a half years had passed since Charles Langley's death.

All those years gave Russell Weinberger time to think. For some of that time, the Commonwealth surely must have feared that its case against Rodriguez had slipped away—if his confession remained inadmissible, nothing linked him to the killing. Weinberger was offered a deal to testify against his friend— years later, he claimed that the offer had been for three years in prison, and he wanted the deal back—but when the Superior Court decided the Rodriguez confession could be used after all, the equation changed in a dramatic way. Now, in the summer of 1985, the offer to Weinberger was fifteen to thirty years; if he didn't take it, prosecutors had his own carefully signed confession, and were going to seek the death penalty. Pennsylvania hadn't executed anyone since 1962, but its death row was growing quickly, and Philadelphia was sending more than its share of inmates there. If he was lucky enough to avoid the electric chair, Weinberger was a likely candidate for a life sentence without the possibility of parole, which was the mandatory punishment for a murder that took place during a robbery.

Whether out of fear of execution or of a life sentence without hope of release, Weinberger decided to deal his way out of the jam. Six months before the scheduled trial, he agreed to serve as a witness against his drinking buddy by pleading guilty to third-degree murder, robbery, and conspiracy in exchange for the fifteen-to-thirty-year sentence. The only condition was that he testify truthfully.

Anthony Sylvanus made his formal confession to the Langley killing in 2001, twenty years, two months, and twenty days after the doctor's death. By that time, Detective Suminski had passed away. Two Philadelphia detectives were present for the confession, as were Sylvanus's public defenders—the commonwealth had already agreed to offer a life sentence for the crime—and the interview took place in the more neutral Criminal Justice Center rather than the police homicide unit. Sylvanus calmly detailed the crime, adding that he had confessed his transgressions to a priest some time before his fingerprint alerted police.

Did he know Felix Rodriguez? Not by his last name, but Sylvanus knew a Felix from the neighborhood. In 1981, when both of them were in the county jail, they had run into each other. Sylvanus had asked Rodriguez what he was in for, and Rodriguez told him he'd been accused of a homicide somewhere on Kensington Avenue where a guy was killed in his store. Sylvanus assumed he was talking about the Langley robbery and murder; even twenty years later, he remembered the exchange:

Q: Did you tell him that you robbed that store?
A: No.
Q: Did you know that it was a doctor's office?
A: I knew, but Felix never mentioned anything along those lines that it was a doctor's office.
Q: Why didn't you tell him?
A: 'Cause I was facing serious charges already. It was stupid. I didn't care if he took the fall or not. Better him than me.

When the statement was concluded, Sylvanus signed the bottom of every page. An error appeared on page three, and he initialed there as well. One last thing was on the detectives' minds.

Q: Are you aware that people are incarcerated for this crime?

A: Yes, when I first confessed to this murder, you came back and said there is a problem, that someone else was arrested for this crime.

Q: We explained to you earlier that two people confessed to this crime and were sentenced to prison. Can you explain that?

A: They were either crazy or stupid.

Anthony Sylvanus may have been joking, but he wasn't far off when he commented that only a crazy or stupid person would admit to a crime he hadn't committed. False confessions are often obtained from those suspects most vulnerable to suggestibility and compliance; juveniles and adults suffering from intellectual disability predominate the list of known exonerees who falsely confessed. In the case of *Atkins v. Virginia*, the U.S. Supreme Court, while barring the death penalty for intellectually disabled people, expressly noted their greater likelihood of falsely confessing, and thus facing "a special risk of wrongful execution."

Russell Weinberger turned out to be intellectually disabled, with an IQ score that placed him in the lowest one percent of the population. Perhaps Detective Suminski knew this—at the very least, he might have had his suspicions when Weinberger spelled *Cumberland* without an *e* or an *a*. On the other hand, some such confessors come to believe in their own guilt. Had Weinberger convinced himself that he was guilty of Langley's murder? The evidence isn't clear. A few years after the trial was over and he had been given the fifteen-to-thirty-year sentence he had bargained for, Weinberger complained about the deal he had received—not that he had confessed to a crime he didn't commit, or that the police had framed him. His complaint was that he should have been given the three-to-ten-year sentence he had initially been offered. But in the late '90s,

when he came up for parole, Weinberger professed his innocence and was turned down. Members of the parole board felt
that he had "failed to take responsibility for the crime."

The jury trial of Felix Rodriguez finally got under way in
August 1985. Just as the death penalty had hung over Russell
Weinberger's head, so too did Rodriguez now face execution
were he to be convicted of first-degree murder. By any analysis,
the case against him was strong, with his signed confession
and the corroborating signed confession of his co-defendant,
Weinberger, who was now also a witness against him. Although a witness who testifies for a deal is generally considered
unreliable—thought to be a "polluted source" whose testimony
jurors are told to accept with extreme caution—Weinberger
had not pleaded guilty in exchange for probation or some un-
conscionably lenient sentence. Rather, he had accepted fifteen
years in state prison, which surely lent him some credibility.
Who in his right mind would take such a deal if he weren't
guilty?

No discussion of Weinberger's intellectual impairment arose
while he was on the stand. Neither the defense attorney nor
the prosecutor asked whether he could read or spell. Neither
established that he had been in special education. No one appears to have raised an eyebrow when Weinberger, asked what
language Rodriguez spoke, answered, "American."

Although the star witness's impairments were not exposed
at the trial, some inconsistencies you might not expect in a
robbery-murder case still arose. Weinberger claimed to have
taken Langley's wallet, which contained $15 or $20; Rodriguez
claimed that he was the one who took the wallet, finding $120
in it. But these discrepancies did not sidetrack the jury members, who appear to have believed the central fact of both
confessions, which was that neither perpetrator intended to
kill Langley. Felix Rodriguez was convicted of second-degree

murder, which in Pennsylvania is a killing that takes place during the course of a felony (in this case, robbery). He was sentenced to mandatory life in prison without the possibility of parole.

When Anthony Sylvanus confessed to his string of murders, he told the police that he had committed the last two with a juvenile named Raymond Ortiz. A week later, the police brought Ortiz into homicide, and he quickly admitted his role in the robbery-murder of eighty-seven-year-old Vincent Morelli in his own home, a crime that had happened five days before Langley's killing. During the next month, both Sylvanus and Ortiz, separately and with their lawyers present, confessed to the Langley case. Neither man was threatened or coerced. The police did not feed them information. "He provided details that only someone who was there would know," Ortiz's lawyer said not long after his client's confession.

So the Commonwealth of Pennsylvania had a problem: four men had confessed to a crime only two had committed. Almost a year later, Sylvanus pleaded guilty to four of the five murders he had admitted to for four consecutive life sentences. No question remained that he was guilty of the crimes; the judge who sentenced Sylvanus noted that he wanted to plead guilty because he did it. "He was truthfully and candidly admitting to something he had done. I was 100 percent convinced." When offered the chance to allocute, this is what Sylvanus said:

> Your Honor, I would just like to say that this proceeding has been long overdue; that [to] the victims' surviving family members, if any of them are here today, I would like to apologize for my past actions; that there's no justification or excuse for what I've done. And that I know that can't bring them back, but if there's a God in heaven, I'm

quite sure that I will also stand before our creator and be judged for what I have done.

I intend to sleep better at night [now] that this has finally come to an end, and you have any interests at heart and I pray that we all can sleep well, you know, without me ever being a future member of society.

I know what I've done was wrong, and I accept that. And whatever judgment comes down on me today, I accept that as well.

Raymond Ortiz pleaded guilty as well. Since he was only sixteen at the time of the crime, and was pretty clearly following the older Sylvanus, he received a five-year sentence for the killing of Vincent Morelli. Neither man was ever charged with Langley's murder. Perhaps the Commonwealth of Pennsylvania thought it unseemly to charge two new men with a crime—even if they were clearly guilty—when two others had confessed, been convicted, and spent years in prison for the same crime.

Anthony Sylvanus's allocution comprised his last public words. He was forty-seven years old at the time of his guilty plea, and met his creator sooner than his life expectancy would have dictated. On a Friday afternoon in August 2009, seven and a half years after being sentenced to four consecutive life sentences, he committed suicide by jumping off the third tier of his housing unit at the state prison in Huntingdon, Pennsylvania.

What about Weinberger and Rodriguez, the two innocent men still in prison? Everyone understood that they needed to be released, but law enforcement couldn't simply open the prison gate. Lawyers had to be involved, and procedures had to be followed, and in the end it was even more complicated than that.

The district attorney's office wasn't objecting to their release—not exactly, anyway. But again a lie-detector test entered the equation, this time a test allegedly flunked by Sylvanus and Ortiz—apparently the machine wasn't certain they were telling the truth when they confessed they had killed Langley. The commonwealth wasn't claiming that a test failed by two obviously guilty men was going to change its mind about Weinberger and Rodriguez; but no district attorney's office likes to admit it has made a mistake, especially when such an admission might expose the process to serious questions and, even worse, serious liability. So the failed tests, if that's what they were, opened up a third option. The commonwealth said it had no objection to granting the men a new trial; nor did it object to releasing the men. But first each of them had to plead *nolo contendere*, meaning that, in this case, neither man was contesting the evidence of his own false confession. That way, the two men who committed the murder would be in prison, albeit for different crimes; the two innocent men, having spent more than two decades in prison for a crime they didn't commit, would be released; and the Commonwealth of Pennsylvania wouldn't have to say it was sorry.

On September 20, 2002, twenty-one and a half years after their arrests, Russell Weinberger and Felix Rodriguez were formally sentenced to the time they had already served in prison for Charles Langley's murder, and declared free to go. When asked by the judge if either man had anything to say, Weinberger demurred. Rodriguez said, "I want to say thanks."

The judge congratulated the district attorney's office for uncovering, investigating, and rectifying "an injustice." Both defense attorneys, appointed by the court to essentially stand next to the defendants because the Constitution required it, commended the prosecutors as well—Rodriguez's lawyer even went so far as to point out that the district attorney's office rarely got good press when they helped "right what well could have been a wrong." The judge noted that no members of the press were in the courtroom, but that they surely would have been there if the case had been a "matter about which something critical might be written about any aspect of the criminal-justice system." No apology was issued to either man for his wrongful incarceration during the proceedings, which took up forty-eight pages of court transcript. Everyone seemed to be under the impression that the criminal justice system had acquitted itself well. No one mentioned false confessions; nor did anyone show any interest in possible remedies to minimize such problems in the future.

Experts like Leo and Kassin recommend a series of reforms that might reduce the risk of wrongful conviction: orienting the police interrogation model away from "confrontational" and toward "investigative"; placing limits on the length of interrogations; precluding the presentation of false evidence to an accused person as real evidence of his guilt; eliminating implicit promises of leniency; and implementing special protections for vulnerable populations such as juveniles and those with cognitive or psychological impairments. Above all is the recommendation that police departments videotape interrogations in their entirety. Slowly but surely, progressive prosecutors and police commissioners are implementing these reforms. Nineteen years after Weinberger and Rodriguez were released from their wrongful prison terms, Philadelphia now videotapes all interrogations between detectives and defendants from beginning to end.

The building at 2520 Kensington Avenue is no longer an optometrist's office—now it is the Wok Fusion Chinese takeout restaurant. To the north is the Hasty Beer Distributor; to the south, a nail salon called Crystal's. The El roars by every three and a half minutes.

Just as the doctor's office has disappeared, so has the ability to reconstruct the injustice that led to the wrongful incarceration of two men for more than two decades. Detective Suminski is dead, as is Anthony Sylvanus. Russell Weinberger has passed as well; he died from cirrhosis of the liver in 2011. His sister, Elaine Weinberger, was still staggered by the case, and what it did to her brother. What might cause an innocent man to confess to murder? To accept fifteen to thirty years in prison and testify against his best friend? "You have to understand: He was slow. He couldn't read or write," she said. "He thought if he went to trial he might get the death penalty, and he was afraid of that, I guess." Russell never wanted to talk about the case with Elaine, and she didn't push him. "He said he didn't remember all that much. When I would ask him, he would just say, 'I never did it, I never did it.'"

One man was left to tell the tale. Years after his release from prison, Felix Rodriguez walked with a cane. He looked fifteen years older than his state identification said he should. He had suffered a stroke and his speech was slurred, but his memory had not dulled. On the subject of the case, he said "they" did this and "they" did that, but when asked to clarify who "they" were, he said, "Detective Suminski."

"First they showed me pictures of the dead guy. I started to cry. I said I didn't do that. That's when they slapped me on the back of my head, said 'They gonna put you in the electric chair.' So I signed the statement. I knew it might be bad, but I didn't know what to do. I'd never been in real trouble before. I signed the statement 'cause they said I could go home." He shook his head and looked to the ground. "People got no business deciding who lives and dies," he said.

Rodriguez was asked about his friend, and the experience of hearing him admit to the murder, saying under oath that Rodriguez did it with him. How could Weinberger have done that? "You have to understand: I was never mad at Russell. Even now I'm not. Me and him grew up together. He was scared, and he was slow anyway. I knew how he felt. I was scared too."

We read about people who have suffered grievous loss through no fault of their own and yet take life's fate with equanimity. Felix Rodriguez was not one of those people. He blamed the police: "They knew I didn't do this; they just scared us." Only once did his veneer crack, when the conversation turned to loss. His mother had passed away in his seventh year of incarceration. "This killed her," he said of his time in prison.

Then he put his head down and cried. "They let me go to her funeral," he said. "I got a lawyer to file something for me, and they let me go. They put cuffs on my hands and legs. There were guards on each side of me. That's how I went to my mom's funeral." Then he stopped crying. He had outlived the detective who put him in prison, and the man whose confession let him out, and even the friend he went there with. But he had not outlived that memory. There are some things you don't outlive.

8

A Descending Spiral

In the summer of 2020, after considerable bluster from Pennsylvania Avenue about executing drug dealers and school shooters and MS-13 members, the federal government ended an unspoken seventeen-year moratorium on capital punishment by killing three men in one week at the federal death row in Terre Haute, then others as the summer and fall wore on. This paroxysm of executions distracted from the reality that the death penalty has been in a long and steady decline. Executions and death sentences in the United States have dropped more than 75 percent from their highs of two decades ago, and there is no evidence to suggest these trends will reverse themselves. Still, there is a steady drip-drip-drip of state-sanctioned killing, almost entirely in a handful of southern states, and many participants in the criminal justice system, including several members of the Supreme Court, appear to be wondering when it will all end.

Some cases seem tailor-made to hurry the discussion along, and Texas's long-grinding case against Andre Thomas is one of them. Thomas's trial and appeals paint a harrowing portrait of mental illness and an unfathomable crime: obsessed with religiosity, he kills his family, removes their hearts with separate knives to avoid contamination, and takes the organs home in his pockets. Then, following a horribly literal reading of the Bible, he removes both of his eyes. An earlier essay in this collection ("How Crazy Is Too Crazy to Be Executed?") tells the tale.

Thomas has been blind for more than a decade now, and Texas continues to push for his execution. But over the course of several oral arguments in 2018 and 2020 before the Fifth Circuit Court of Appeals, federal judges have hinted they are troubled by more than just Thomas's psychoses. In short, his severe mental illness has overshadowed a far more insidious aspect of his trial: three members of the jury and an alternate juror believed that his interracial marriage with the victim violated the racial tenets they lived by.

How jurors with those beliefs sat on Andre Thomas's jury is a fair question to ask. Was this a mistake brought on by sloppiness or overwork or just the harried nature of a capital jury trial? It wasn't. The lawyers were well aware of the racial implications of the crime, and they included an item on the jury questionnaire about interracial marriage. Four potential jurors indicated they were "opposed" or "strongly opposed" to such pairings. One might think that such answers would raise alarms on the defense side of the room, but Thomas's court-appointed defense lawyers didn't ask three of the four jurors a single follow-up question about race to try to disqualify them, nor did they use a peremptory strike to have them removed.

Those three jurors, and nine others, rejected an insanity defense and voted to give Andre Thomas the death penalty. When the case moved inevitably into the post-conviction stage, the same defense attorneys who had failed to keep Thomas off death row proved even less helpful. They gave prosecutors and Thomas's appellate lawyers contradictory statements regarding their own conduct at trial, and they used virtually identical language to explain their failure to probe deeper into the jurors' antipathy toward mixed marriages: We "questioned them to the extent necessary for us to request a strike for cause or make a decision to use a strike against them."

One of the lawyers went even further, accusing Thomas's appellate attorneys of race-baiting and claiming that "the prosecutors and jurors are being accused of racial prejudice without any basis in the record." It seems that the jurors' sworn comments regarding interracial marriage—"I don't believe God intended for this," "We should stay with our bloodline," and "[It is] harmful for the children involved because they don't have a specific race to belong to"—did not meet their threshold for racial bias.

Thomas's appeals were roundly rejected by Texas state courts, so he moved on to the federal district court in eastern Texas. There, without explanation, his case was passed from one judge to another to a third, until it finally came to rest where it had begun, with Judge Michael H. Schneider, a 2004 appointee of President George W. Bush.

Schneider made short shrift of the mental health and racial bias claims presented by Thomas's appellate attorneys. Relying on procedural rules ushered in after the Republican takeover of the House of Representatives in 1994, he followed the state courts' lead by attributing credibility to the statements Thomas's original lawyers had given to the prosecution after his trial, while ignoring the contradictory statements those lawyers had provided six months earlier to the lawyers representing Thomas in his appeals.

Schneider ruled that the failure of Thomas's original defense lawyers to press some jurors on perceived racial biases "was simply a matter of trial strategy." But overlooking the obvious racial implications of the case would have been a curious strategy indeed. Certainly the lead prosecutor didn't when he concluded his closing argument for execution by asking the all-white jury whether they were willing to risk Thomas "asking your daughter out, or your granddaughter out?"

As for Thomas's competence to stand trial after gouging his eye out and being committed to the state mental hospital, Schneider sided with the Texas courts in crediting B. Thomas Gray, a clinical psychologist who noted that Thomas had been diagnosed as "malingering" and that he "may engage in gestures or behaviors, including possibly those involving self-harm, in a bid to appear more seriously mentally ill than he is." Might the doctor still think Thomas was attempting to appear more seriously mentally ill than he actually was after he removed his second eyeball and ate it? Schneider's opinion does not raise the question.

The ruling left no doubt about Schneider's views: he denied every issue raised by the defense and declared that no "reasonable jurists" could even debate the merits of Thomas's claims. His seventy-seven-page opinion was published on September 19, 2016—Schneider retired from the federal bench twelve days later.

But the legal winds soon shifted at least slightly in Thomas's favor. In 2017, the Supreme Court handed down two important decisions about discrimination in a criminal law context. Although neither related directly to Thomas's fate, both cases showed that the court was finally taking a clear-eyed look at the racial elephant in the courtroom.

In *Peña-Rodriguez v. Colorado*, the high court reversed a sexual assault conviction wherein a juror had condemned the defendant during deliberations "because he's Mexican and Mexican men take whatever they want . . . nine times out of ten Mexican men were guilty of being aggressive toward women and young girls." Unlike the Thomas jurors, who had expressed racial animosity and were not questioned about it by his defense lawyers, the biased juror in *Peña-Rodriguez* did not reveal his prejudice during jury selection.

The second Supreme Court decision, *Buck v. Davis*, involved Duane Buck, a Texas death row inmate whose own lawyer put a psychologist on the stand to testify about his client's likelihood of committing criminal acts of violence that would constitute a continuing threat to society. This expert witness concluded that Buck probably would not engage in further violent conduct, but that because he was Black, there was an elevated probability he would.

Chief Justice John Roberts, recognizing that Buck may have been sentenced to death in part because of his race, wrote that this was "a disturbing departure from a basic premise of our criminal justice system: Our law punishes people for what they do, not who they are. Dispensing punishment on the basis of an immutable characteristic flatly contravenes this guiding principle." This was a harsh reversal of the Fifth Circuit's opinion, which held that Buck had "not made out even a minimal showing" that his case was exceptional.

Like Schneider in the Thomas case, the Fifth Circuit in *Buck* had determined that no reasonable jurist could argue that Buck's claim of racial bias had merit. Thomas's next appellate stop was that very same Fifth Circuit. Had they learned anything from *Buck v. Davis*? The first oral argument suggested that they had.

In his book *The Supreme Court*, the late Chief Justice William Rehnquist wrote about an 1824 case, *Gibbons v. Ogden*, that involved five days of oral argument before the court. Appeals courts these days rarely allow more than an hour, and so it was in the Thomas case. Still, the racial bias of the jurors was of significant interest to the three-judge panel. When one of the judges asked about the claim by one of Thomas's trial lawyers that he had avoided questioning those jurors further for fear of creating animosity, Thomas's appellate attorney was prepared:

> He does say that in his second affidavit, which of course is diametrically contrary to the first affidavit he submitted, in which he said, "There was no intentional strategy, I simply just didn't ask." What we know here is that these questions were posed to the jurors . . . in the first place precisely because the interracial dynamics of the facts in this case were so palpable that it was recognized that this was an important question that needed to be asked. So it's not a reasonable strategy to then say, "Well, I don't want to inject race into the discussion." Race was already injected into the discussion, and these jurors gave extremely troubling responses.

When it was the assistant attorney general's turn to argue, a serious misstatement in the state's brief was exposed. The prosecution had erroneously claimed all the jurors at issue were questioned further about their views on interracial marriage:

> Judge Stephen Higginson: On page 36 of your brief, you say trial counsel extensively questioned all four [jurors] regarding whether Thomas and [the victim's] race would impact their ability to remain impartial. You said all four indicated it would not. You didn't give a record [citation]. Is it your position that, when I look at the transcript, that trial counsel questioned [the two jurors in question] as to whether or not their race would impact the ability to remain impartial?
> Prosecutor: At this point, I have to admit that that was a mistake.

Judge: It's a pretty significant mistake.

Prosecutor: It is, Your Honor.

Not surprisingly, Thomas's severe mental illness came up prominently. When the state attempted to portray the killings as "revenge and obsession," Higginson was not having it. "It seems like the state admits, and certainly the defense insists, that the defendant was psychotic," he said. "You're saying that this was a revenge killing . . . [and that] does seem to be missing the greater point, that even you acknowledge, that this is a matter of a person who was psychotic at the time."

Thomas's attorney ended her presentation by explaining that the trial lawyers had failed to provide an accurate portrayal of her profoundly disturbed client: "What [the jury] should have seen, and what would have gravely affected their evaluation of whether he deserved to die, was that as a little boy he was suffering the effects of this organic mental illness. He needed help. He never got it."

Higginson concluded the hearing with an understatement. "It's an important set of questions for us to resolve," he said. Then, only two days later, the Fifth Circuit panel issued an order acknowledging what was painfully obvious to anyone who had been in the courtroom for the argument: That "reasonable jurists could disagree" on the race and mental illness aspects of the case. The judges then asked both sides to brief them further on those issues.

The order amounted to a rare glimmer of hope for Thomas, who by then was entering his thirteenth year on death row; but the Fifth Circuit has not issued a final opinion, and Texas is still trying to execute him. The state's lead argument regarding the racist jurors is dizzyingly circular: since Thomas's trial attorneys didn't object to those jurors, his new attorneys can't complain about it now. In other words, the lawyers who thought the jurors opposed to interracial marriage weren't racist were responsible for objecting to any racist jurors.

The state's perspective on Thomas's glaring mental illness is simple—the crime itself was so awful, no evidence of his background could have saved him; and besides, the lawyers did the best they could. To prove this last point, the state's brief unintentionally highlights the strongly genetic aspect of Thomas's troubles. His mother refused to cooperate with the defense, and failed to appear at her son's trial. She had been questioned by the grand jury, but when asked to say "some good things" about Andre, could only answer "he is my son." What did she think should happen to him? "It is God's will," she responded.

But for now it is Texas's will obscuring the racism of the jurors and the profound mental illness of the perpetrator. While justice purports to be blind, does anyone believe it to be served by executing Andre Thomas?

9

Trials and Errors

It may have appeared coincidental when, on August 23, 2016, two startling events transpired in separate high-profile Philadelphia murder cases. Anthony Wright, facing a jury for the second time after DNA revealed the probability of another perpetrator, was acquitted of the rape and murder of an elderly woman after a short deliberation. And James Dennis, on death row for the robbery and murder of a young woman, was granted a new trial by the Third Circuit Court of Appeals based on evidence hidden by the Commonwealth of Pennsylvania at the time of his arrest. Both murders had occurred within a four-day period in October 1991; both investigations had involved the same two homicide detectives.

Was it really a coincidence? Vladimir Nabokov, one of the twentieth century's greatest writers, spent much of his literary career navigating the rough waters between crime, detection, and punishment. He wrote: "A certain man once lost a diamond cufflink in the wide blue sea, and twenty years later, on the exact day, a Friday apparently, he was eating a large fish—but there was no diamond inside. That's what I like about coincidence." Cufflinks remain lost in real life, too. There are no coincidences in criminal justice stories, only explanations waiting to be discovered.

The Philadelphia District Attorney's Office was not interested in explanations, however. Reiterating its belief that Wright and Dennis were guilty, the office rebuffed allegations of wrongdoing. "If Mr. Wright's legal team, or anyone else, has evidence of specific misconduct by any Philadelphia police officer, they should report it to us. As in the past, we will review it and proceed accordingly," a spokesperson announced. He did not mention that the Commonwealth was already in possession of such evidence, and had been since 1994.

During the afternoon hours of October 19, 1991, seventy-seven-year-old Louise Talley was found nude and on the floor, stabbed to death in her North Philadelphia home. After a flurry of interviews with police and local residents, law enforcement's attention quickly focused on Anthony Wright, a twenty-year-old who lived nearby. Fewer than twenty-four hours after the victim had been discovered, Wright was sitting in room 104 of the Police Administration Building; by the time he left the room a few hours later, he had signed a statement that would put him in prison for the next twenty-five years. One of the men who questioned him was Manuel Santiago, a detective in his seventh year in homicide.

The statement, neither audio-recorded nor videotaped and in the handwriting of one of the detectives, was quite damning:

> I knocked on her front door and when she unlocked the door and opened it a little I like just barged into her house . . . [A]s we went through the kitchen I picked up this knife that I saw by the kitchen sink. Anyway, I forced her to go upstairs and I took her into the middle bedroom and when we got in there I told her to take her clothes off

because I was going to tie her up. She just kept begging me not to hurt her. She took her clothes off and then she started to struggle and that's when I stabbed her.

While the confession itself was probably enough to convict Wright, there was more. When asked what he was wearing when he killed the victim, he said he'd had on a Chicago Bulls sweatshirt, a pair of blue jeans with suede on them, and Fila sneakers. The following night, a homicide detective named Frank Jastrzembski and other police officers recovered those exact clothes under the mattress in Wright's bedroom, acting on a search warrant obtained by Jastrzembski; the sweatshirt and jeans were splattered with the victim's blood. Other witnesses identified Wright as having been at or near the scene of the crime, and connected him to some televisions stolen from the house. The case was closed in a single day.

Two days after Wright was arrested for the murder of Louise Talley, Detectives Santiago and Jastrzembski were busy on another murder investigation less than three miles away. A high school student named Chedell Williams had been shot and killed after two men had approached her and a friend and demanded that they "give me your fucking earrings." Acting on a rumor that "Jimmy" Dennis—a young man from a housing project a few miles away—had committed the crime, the police, led by Jastrzembski, ultimately found three eyewitnesses who identified him in a photo display, an in-person lineup, and a preliminary hearing. There was no physical evidence and no confession, but three eyewitnesses made for a strong case. Dennis, too, was arrested.

The Wright and Dennis cases followed the usual path of notorious Philadelphia murders. The DA's office sought the death penalty in each. One year later, Dennis was convicted of first-degree murder and sent to Pennsylvania's death row.

Eight months after that, Wright was also convicted, but when the jury could not decide between life and death, he was sentenced to life without the possibility of parole. Appeals would follow for both, years of them, and detectives Santiago and Jastrzembski moved on to new homicide investigations.

In May 1993, less than a month before Anthony Wright was sentenced to spend the rest of his life in prison, Santiago became the assigned detective in the killing of Japelle McCray, which occurred during a street craps game in North Philadelphia. The police soon found a witness, a young man who identified himself as David Glenn. He gave a statement that "Percy" had shot the victim, but he did not know Percy's last name. Further investigation suggested that "Percy" might be Percy St. George. The police, having only a single witness, went looking for this David Glenn to confirm they were on the right track.

Perhaps the McCray case wasn't a priority, or the homicide division was busier than usual that summer. For whatever reason, it was several months before Detective Santiago brought Glenn into the police station; there, the witness acknowledged that he had previously told the police about "Percy." When the detective showed him a photo array, Glenn signed a photograph identifying Percy St. George as the man he had seen kill Japelle McCray. There was no physical evidence and no confession, and only one eyewitness this time—in short, the case was not nearly as strong as the Wright or Dennis cases. Nevertheless, the police arrested Percy St. George, relying on the veracity and accuracy of David Glenn. The Defender Association of Philadelphia was appointed to represent St. George.

Glenn proved to be a reluctant witness at the preliminary hearing. This is not unusual in homicide cases; witnesses rarely come forward enthusiastically. But Glenn was more averse than the typically disinclined witness—not only did he claim he had seen nothing, he insisted that he had not even made the initial statement about "Percy." When asked why he had identified Percy St. George as the killer when he hadn't even seen the crime, he sounded like the sixteen-year-old he was: "[Santiago] told me that I could get locked up, so I was scared, because I had never been locked up before."

Such recantations are commonplace in criminal court-rooms, and detectives are adept at overcoming them. Santiago testified under oath that it was Glenn who'd admitted to making the initial statement saying "Percy" did it, and Glenn who'd picked out the Percy St. George photo "almost immediately." That was enough—St. George would stand trial for murder. Jastrzembski also took a statement from the victim's twin sister, who identified Glenn as the eyewitness she had talked to immediately after her brother's shooting. Single and reluctant witness or not, the Philadelphia district attorney decided to seek the death penalty.

There were some good reasons to believe Glenn rather than Santiago. The two statements—one he denied making at all, the other that he said had been coerced—showed different dates of birth and different home addresses for Glenn. There was also a little quirk in the signature on the first statement: the *i* in *David* had a circle instead of a point. If Glenn had not given the first statement, who had? He swore under oath that it was his friend, another sixteen-year-old named Inmon Goggans.

A short investigation followed. Short, because when asked separately by the defense and the prosecution whether he had given the first statement to the police and used the name David Glenn, Goggans immediately admitted that he had. Why? He was worried about being arrested on some bench warrants, so he used his friend's name to avoid detection. Goggans said he had not actually seen the killing at all; when the police rounded him up as a witness, he wanted to get out of there as quickly as possible, so he told them what they'd wanted to hear.

A year after St. George's arrest, one thing was clear beyond question: sixteen-year-old David Glenn, who had entered police headquarters having seen and done nothing, left admitting to a statement he hadn't given, and identifying the perpetrator of a crime he hadn't witnessed. Someone was going to have to explain how this could have happened. Had Detective Santiago coerced a teenager to wrongly identify someone in a capital murder investigation? Had Detective Jastrzembski encouraged the victim's sister to misidentify the tall and gawky David Glenn for the short and squat Inmon Goggans?

On October 7, 1994, exactly one year after Percy St. George's preliminary hearing, another hearing was scheduled, this one at the request of the defense to "bar prosecution based on due process violations." Santiago was subpoenaed to testify, but his attorney responded instead. Calling the allegations against his client "bold, unsupported, and scurrilous," the lawyer nonetheless pointed out that the detective would be "compelled to assert his Fifth Amendment privilege." Two other detectives involved in the investigation also took the Fifth, leaving the commonwealth without evidence or witnesses. The capital murder charge against St. George was dismissed, and the hearing was canceled. None of the three detectives was charged with a crime, and all remained on the police force after the case was closed. No explanation has ever been offered for why three Philadelphia detectives, two of whom were assigned to the homicide unit, would assert their Fifth Amendment rights in a case where they were the investigators rather than the investigated.

* * *

Serious criminal appeals are the exact opposite of trials. They occur not as singular events, but usually span decades and jurisdictions. The vast majority disappear with yesterday's newspaper, never to be read again. If some new truth does emerge during the appellate process, it often arrives buried in procedural minutiae. Thus it was with the Wright and Dennis cases.

After more than a decade in prison, Wright began petitioning the court to analyze the DNA of the bodily fluids recovered from the victim. Although such testing had occurred in criminal cases as early as the late 1980s, it was still relatively rare at the time of Wright's trial. Even when testing became common, the prosecution routinely fought it in older cases, and courts often refused to order it. The logic was Heller-ian. In order to get post-conviction testing, the applicant had to show that the results, if exculpatory, would prove him innocent. This was the conundrum facing Anthony Wright: his alleged confession to Detective Santiago could not be disproven by DNA.

After a judge in Philadelphia rejected his request, he looked to the Pennsylvania Superior Court, which turned him down as well. Another three years passed until the state Supreme Court—citing a number of wrongful convictions that involved confessions—reversed the Superior Court, and it took another several years after that until the testing was complete. By then it was 2014, and Wright was entering his third decade of incarceration.

The DNA results proved to be a bombshell. Not only was there no physical evidence placing Anthony Wright at the scene of the crime, but the sperm found in the victim's vagina and rectum turned out to be that of a small-time criminal and crack addict named Ronnie Byrd, who had lived near the victim's house and subsequently died in a South Carolina prison.

Remarkably, the name "Ronnie Byrd" did not appear in the 1991 police reports. And there was more—the bloody clothes Jastrzembski claimed to have seized from Wright's bedroom did not have Wright's DNA on them, but the victim's; the locations of the trace evidence made it clear that *she* had been wearing the clothes. The case seemed to have collapsed under the weight of incontrovertible evidence. But the Philadelphia District Attorney's Office had a different perspective. Noting that there was "utterly overwhelming evidence of [Wright's] guilt," the prosecution claimed the DNA simply raised the "possibility of a second perpetrator." This was news to anyone who watched the first trial—there had been no mention of a second perpetrator then. Even the alleged confession hadn't referenced another person. But the commonwealth was undaunted. The DA's office would not oppose a new trial for Anthony Wright. But prosecutors still professed that he was guilty, and they still intended to prove it.

Prosecutors and defense attorneys alike have noted that jurors expect to see DNA evidence in every murder case, a perception court-watchers have dubbed the "CSI Effect." In reality, a 2010 study showed that DNA evidence exists in less than 5 percent of homicide investigations. Wrongful convictions that are overturned based on DNA evidence represent only a sliver of people who are unjustly imprisoned in the United States. The Innocence Project reports that 71 percent of DNA exonerations have also involved witness identifications that later proved to be incorrect, but prosecutors and judges are far less likely to acknowledge the possible injustice of a misidentification when there is no DNA to confirm it. Those fighting to prove their innocence without the benefit of DNA evidence are leaning into a very stiff wind.

James Dennis had no genetic testing available to exonerate

him after his conviction. What he did have was a receipt for a welfare check, one that belonged to a woman who'd been on the same bus as Dennis, four miles from where the crime had occurred. When he was arrested, he told the police he had seen this woman at the time of the murder, but she testified against him at trial: she said she had seen Dennis on the bus two hours after the crime, negating his alibi. The woman based her testimony on the recollection that she had noticed him about an hour after cashing her welfare check. Detectives prompted her memory with a receipt stamped 13:03, which she mistakenly understood to be 3:03 p.m. The prosecution did not correct her, nor did they provide the receipt to the defense. In the eyes of the jury, Dennis had lied about his whereabouts at the time of the murder.

The Pennsylvania Supreme Court denied his appeal, finding the receipt irrelevant and noting "the overwhelming evidence" of Dennis's guilt. He returned to that same court three more times over the next thirteen years, in each instance heading back to death row with more evidence of innocence and commonwealth misconduct, and less hope for a new trial. In his last state appeal, Dennis established that the main eyewitness had told the victim's aunt and uncle she recognized the perpetrator from her high school, a school he had not attended. That statement had been kept from Dennis's lawyer at trial. The court was not impressed, however; there were two other eyewitnesses who had positively identified him.

It was the beginning of 2011. Within a month the Pennsylvania Supreme Court had cleared the way for DNA testing in the Wright case, but had rebuffed Dennis's claim that he had been wrongly identified. While Wright began to prepare for a new trial, Dennis looked to the federal courts for relief. As would soon be revealed, the case against him was far weaker than the previous appeals had indicated.

*   *   *

Any lawyer in the criminal justice system is familiar with the case of *Brady v. Maryland*. Indeed, the opinion is so ingrained in the day-to-day functioning of the law that attorneys on both sides of the aisle simply refer to "*Brady* evidence"—material in the possession of the state that must be provided to the defense because it is "favorable to an accused." On its face, it is a clear-cut rule, but criminal lawyers know better. As the late Supreme Court Justice John Marshall Harlan said in a very different context, "one man's vulgarity is another's lyric." In other words, *favorable* is subject to interpretation.

There is an additional artifice to the *Brady* rule: the decision about what is "favorable" is not made by a neutral party, but by the prosecution. There is thus a "fox guarding the henhouse" quality to the process, and many legal commentators have questioned the efficacy of placing this obligation on the prosecution. James Dennis certainly had reason to believe the Philadelphia District Attorney's Office was taking a very narrow view of its responsibility.

The welfare receipt and the statement that the perpetrator had attended the victim's high school were important—any defense attorney would have wanted such information. But there was more that hadn't been turned over. Ten days after the murder, an inmate in a local county jail named William Frazier informed the police that a friend had told him that he and two other men had committed the murder in question. Although inmates often try to negotiate their way out of prison by bartering less than dependable material, this statement offered what the law likes to call "indicia of reliability." It included specific details that comported with the evidence the police had already gathered about the murder; it identified a triggerman who fit eyewitnesses' physical description of the perpetrator more closely than James Dennis did; and the confession itself had been overheard by Frazier's aunt, a wholly disinterested witness.

In all, the prosecution withheld six documents relating to Frazier's statement from the defense. The police had taken Frazier seriously—they'd escorted him from the jail on a ride-along, where he pointed out the homes of the people he'd named. He also told them that one of the men "likes to wear sweat suits," a fact that fit the description provided by eyewitnesses. Nevertheless, the commonwealth claimed the Frazier lead was a dead end and thus immaterial. The federal district court made short work of that argument, pointing out that the statement was credible and could not be "passed off as merely a 'fruitless lead' that the prosecution was entitled to keep to itself." The federal court, twenty-two years after the crime, granted Dennis a new trial.

Philadelphia District Attorney Seth Williams was not shamed by the revelation that his office had hidden important evidence. Rather, he was emboldened, condemning the district court's "acceptance of slanted factual allegations." Now it was the DA's turn to take the next step up the appeals ladder. By the time the Third Circuit Court of Appeals reexamined the Dennis prosecution three years later, some old facts were brought into a new light.

It turned out that detectives Santiago and Jastrzembski were more deeply involved in the investigation than the previous appeals indicated. They had followed up Frazier's tip by speaking to one of the three men he'd implicated in the murder. That man had admitted knowing the victim from high school, and to hanging out on the exact same corner where an eyewitnesses said he'd seen one of the alleged perpetrators. Yet the detectives hadn't shown a photo of the man to any of the witnesses, nor had they revealed the information to the defense.

Santiago had also conducted all of the photo displays, just

as he would a few years later with David Glenn in the Percy St. George case. Jastrzembski, meanwhile, said he had seized clothes from Dennis's house, just as he claimed to have done in the Wright case. Although he later testified that those items fit the description of the clothing worn by the perpetrator, the jury never saw the actual garments. According to the detective, the clothes had been thrown in the trash by cleaners.

Two months short of a quarter century after the crime that sent Dennis to death row, the Third Circuit, in a rare *en banc* decision, voted 9–4 to grant him a new trial. Once again, the Philadelphia District Attorney's Office derided the court's decision, stating that it would "determine whether to seek further review on the basis of the compelling dissent by four federal judges, who concluded that the evidence against Dennis remains 'strong.'"

While James Dennis was still fighting for his freedom, Anthony Wright had neared the end of his ordeal. His second trial, handled by the Innocence Project and a top Philadelphia law firm, was shaping up as a very different affair from the first. Not only had DNA evidence cast doubt on the provenance of the clothes allegedly recovered by Detective Jastrzembski, but an entirely new suspect had been introduced into the case. Only one thing remained unchanged—the unrecorded confession taken by Detective Santiago. This time around, the defense argued that the jury should learn about the detective's methods in the Percy St. George case:

> [W]e intend to question [Santiago] regarding allegations of witness coercion and other wrongdoing concerning a statement taken from a material witness in that homicide case. And an alleged coercion of that witness' signing and identifying a photograph in that case. [Also] regarding

the letter written by his attorney dated October 3rd, 1994 . . . in connection with that case . . . that if called to the witness stand regarding that case and not granted full immunity, Detective Santiago would plead the Fifth Amendment rather than testifying in open court.

Nina Morrison, of the Innocence Project, emphasized that the St. George case was "not an everyday isolated accusation of misconduct. [Detective Santiago] was willing to let a capital murder case get dismissed with prejudice rather than take the stand and defend the simple taking of a witness statement."

The prosecution's position was clear, if ironic: Detective Santiago had never been convicted of any crime, and "unconvicted criminal accusations" were never permitted into evidence. Neither side pointed out that Santiago could not possibly have been convicted, since the same prosecutor's office had not even arrested him for his conduct. Nonetheless, the judge refused to allow inquiry into the St. George case.

In the end, though, it didn't matter. "DNA has changed the playing field in criminal justice," Peter Neufeld, the co-founder of the Innocence Project, told the jury. "Now you jurors will level that playing field." In August 2016, after a nine-day trial, the jury deliberated over lunch and then acquitted Anthony Wright. While his lawyers worked to have the paperwork processed for his release, the Wright family shared emotional moments with the jurors, who had remained at the courthouse after their verdict.

"I'm angry," the jury forewoman said. "The evidence was there that he did not commit this crime. The city should never have brought this case. I'm just happy that today's verdict will let Tony move on with the rest of his life." She labeled the statement that Santiago elicited from Wright a "supposed confession."

The defense team called for an independent investigation of all convictions of young Black men who were prosecuted using evidence developed by the detectives in Wright's case. "After the DNA results were known, we have three and a half years where the District Attorney's Office did nothing to reinvestigate this case or find out who Ronnie Byrd was," Neufeld said. "It's absolutely unconscionable and unacceptable."

The Philadelphia prosecutors were not deterred by the quick acquittal. "We believe that the evidence was sufficient to prove Anthony Wright participated in the murder of Louise Talley," the office spokesperson declared, adhering to its new theory that Wright had not acted alone. There was no need for an independent investigation of all convictions of young Black men, the DA's office added, as no evidence of "specific misconduct" had been produced. The fact that three Philadelphia detectives, including the detective who testified about the "supposed confession" by Wright, had taken the Fifth in a separate case, and that the District Attorney's Office had done nothing about it for more than two decades, went unmentioned.

Four months after Anthony Wright went home, James Dennis left death row. Surrounded by a phalanx of lawyers, some of whom had been helping him for decades, he walked into Philadelphia's Criminal Justice Center in a burgundy jumpsuit, short and squat and bald. While the prosecutor still believed him guilty, there was the matter of all those police reports that hadn't been turned over, and the very real chance Dennis might be acquitted as Wright had been. Maybe neither side wanted to take a chance. In any case, Dennis pled no contest to the same charges that had put him in line to be executed, only this time the twenty-five years he had already served paid his bill to the commonwealth. When asked if he had anything to say, he told the judge he'd been in prison all those years for crimes he hadn't committed. "I just want the nightmare to end," he said. An old robbery charge from 1991 was still on his record, but the prosecution agreed to recommend his parole. In May 2017 he left prison for good.

Wright and Dennis spent the Clinton, Bush, and Obama years in prison. But the detectives accused of misconduct in those cases have emerged from the accusations unscathed. Both Santiago and Jastrzembski served as Philadelphia police officers for more than twenty-five years, each spending a decade or more in the homicide division. Santiago went on to be a special agent in the Pennsylvania Attorney General's Office, where he was working at the time of his testimony in the second Wright trial. Jastrzembski spent another seventeen years in private security after leaving the police force, finally retiring in 2015.

The last chapter of this saga has not yet been written. In September 2016, a premier Philadelphia civil rights firm filed a wide-ranging lawsuit against the city and eleven police officers, including Santiago and Jastrzembski. Alleging a conspiracy to deprive Wright of his liberty through a malicious prosecution, the complaint lists a pervasive pattern and practice of unconstitutional transgressions in homicide investigations, including coerced confessions, fabricated false evidence, and withheld exculpatory evidence. Eight other cases involving misconduct are listed, among them the ones involving James Dennis and Percy St. George. One of the many claims alleged in the lawsuit is that Philadelphia and its police department have been "deliberately indifferent" to the need to discipline police officers. The lawsuit is ongoing.

Like all civil claims, the damages sought are monetary. Clocks cannot be turned back, youth cannot be restored. Near the end of his testimony in the Wright trial, Jastrzembski remarked, "It's not TV. This is the real thing." He doesn't need to tell Wright, and Dennis, and St. George. They already know.

10

Stranger in a Strange Land

> In a society in which it is a moral offense to be different
> from your neighbor your only escape is to never let them
> find out.
>
> —Robert Heinlein

The anti-immigration narrative has always been Biblical. Old
Testament. There are allusions to plagues and floods, and an
underlying hysteria that cries out to do something, and to do it
now. When President Trump tweeted about illegal immigrants
pouring into and infesting the United States, we understood,
just as we understood Joseph McCarthy when he spoke about
communists infesting the State Department or the *Daily Mail*
when it wrote of "German Jews pouring into" England to avoid
the Nazis in 1938. That article, by a nameless "Daily Mail Reporter," went on:

> The number of aliens entering this country can be seen
> by the number of prosecutions in recent months. It is very
> difficult for the alien to escape the increasing vigilance of
> the police and port authorities. Even if aliens manage to

break through the defences it is not long before they are caught and deported.

Eighty-three years later the narrative is unchanged. The portentous language—of aliens and escape, vigilance and being caught, prosecutions and port authorities, of invasions by marauding caravans—remains the idiom of today. The asylum seeker, the teenager with his family, the tourist who never left, the family man just looking for a job, all of them are pushed under the same umbrella. All of them are the alien, the illegal. All of them are MS-13.

But what about Clemente Javier Aguirre-Jarquin? When he entered the country illegally from Honduras in 2003 he was not a child brought along by parents, but an adult of twenty-two. Nor had he set about on a law-abiding path that might be a paradigm of the American dream; rather, barely a year after he set foot in Florida he stood accused of the stabbing deaths of two next-door neighbors, a wheelchair-bound mother and her daughter. The daughter had been stabbed one hundred twenty-nine times. All sixty-four bloody shoe impressions capable of comparison from the crime scene matched Aguirre's shoes, and his clothes had both victims' blood on them. He admitted to being in their house and seeing the dead bodies—how could he not?—but he hadn't killed them, he claimed. He was there looking for beer when he had run out of his own after drinking all day.

Why hadn't he called the police to report what he had seen? He was undocumented, and feared being deported. With that evidence, there was little surprise when Aguirre was convicted and given two death sentences.

Clemente Javier Aguirre-Jarquin hadn't sought asylum or overstayed a visa. Instead, he had committed an unspeakable crime, and now the taxpayers were footing his room and board until the time came for his execution. And for the Florida prosecutors who had put him on death row one thing was certain: had the borders been tighter, those two women would still have been alive. Alien, illegal, undocumented, it hardly mattered what you called him. What did matter was that he'd committed two murders, and there was an Old Testament narrative for that as well.

There has always been a strong presumption in criminal justice that the system got it right the first time: that defense lawyers did a competent job, prosecutors acted honorably, judges conducted a fair trial, and juries accurately determined the facts. The reality of the presumption, though, is hard to assess. While popular myth has it that virtually all convictions get reversed through obscure technicalities or a soft-hearted judiciary, the truth is quite the opposite. A 2010 study by the U.S. Department of Justice indicated that less than 12 percent of all appeals granted any relief to the convicted; but that same study showed that death penalty appeals were more than twice as likely to be reversed as felonies or misdemeanors.

Since the stakes are so much higher in capital cases than in even the most serious non-capital homicides, an outsider might speculate that prosecutors are more likely to cut corners and judges more likely to look the other way when they do; or that out-resourced and untrained defense attorneys are simply overwhelmed by the work necessary to do a competent job. Undoubtedly capital cases are subjected to far greater scrutiny than the average felony, and given the much higher reversal rate in those cases it is reasonable to wonder if the death penalty system would pass the government equivalent of a car inspection. The team of lawyers who took over the Aguirre case didn't think so. It was their job to take a fresh look at a crime that had occurred seven years earlier, and they started where most debates regarding innocence or guilt start these days, with questions about deoxyribonucleic acid.

The use of DNA evidence, common in criminal prosecutions since the mid-1990s, was first upheld in a U.S. criminal courtroom in 1987. DNA in that case led to the conviction of a man named Tommie Lee Andrews, and the trial occurred in Orlando, only half an hour from the Seminole County courthouse where Clemente Aguirre was convicted seventeen years later. Yet with the incredibly bloody crime scene left behind from the stabbing of the two women, and the massive amount of physical evidence taken in the investigation of the killings, a surprisingly small amount of DNA testing had been done. Aguirre's new attorneys, claiming that his trial lawyers had been ineffective in not seeking DNA results, asked that the physical evidence be more thoroughly examined.

There were the usual skirmishes between the defense and the prosecution about what should be tested and how it should be done, but in 2012, eight years after the crime itself, results began dripping in. Literally. It turned out there were two drops of blood—one in the kitchen, the other in the living room at the crime scene—that did not belong to either victim. Nor did either drop come from Aguirre. And there were two other interesting facts: the blood was from a female, and that female was likely related to the victims.

There was only one person who fit that profile: Samantha Williams.

Samantha Williams was no stranger to the case. The daughter and granddaughter of the victims, she lived in the trailer home with them; and she had been a central witness against Clemente Aguirre, testifying that several months before the murders she woke at two in the morning to find Aguirre standing over her bed. Screaming at him to leave, she had escorted him out the front door and locked the door behind him. She explained to the police that she had not been there on the night her family was killed, because she had been arguing with her mother.

Instead she had been with her boyfriend, Mark Van Sandt, at his parents' place. Indeed, Van Sandt had been the first to discover the bodies the next morning, when he stopped by to pick up Samantha's work clothes. Since Samantha lived in the house, maybe it wasn't entirely shocking that a few drops of her blood might be found; but the one in the kitchen was particularly troubling, since the testimony from the trial indicated that the kitchen floor had been mopped shortly before the killings had occurred. In any case, the prosecution agreed to compare Samantha's DNA profile to the blood to see if it matched. This was when things started to get interesting.

A few months later, propelled by the knowledge that the two drops of blood appeared to exculpate their client, Aguirre's lawyers filed a motion asking that more evidence be tested for DNA. This time, the prosecution took a very different position:

> The State objects to the additional testing because the testing will not provide evidence of the Defendant's innocence . . . Now the Defendant wants to test items in other areas of the home. The Defendant's position that the individual who committed these murders cut themselves does not make sense . . . The area sought to be tested is basically the living area of Samantha Williams. The fact that her DNA could be located in this area does not exonerate the defendant nor mitigate his sentence.

What prompted the prosecutors to stand in the way of simply testing the evidence in a case in which a man might be executed by the state? Perhaps the answer lay in a motion they had filed in secret only five days earlier. On June 21, 2012, the state's attorneys provided four documents to Jessica Recksiedler, the judge presiding over Aguirre's appeal. The documents were related to what is known in Florida as the "Baker Act," more formally known as the Florida Mental Health Act, and they were turned over *ex parte*, a legal term meaning that only the court would see them. When the judge made those documents available to Aguirre's attorneys two weeks later, the narrative of the case changed dramatically. Or so the attorneys assumed.

To paraphrase Tolstoy, every unhappy immigration story is unhappy in its own way. Surely Clemente Aguirre's experience in Honduras might have made anyone decide to seek a happier life elsewhere. Violence was "the daily bread of the community," noted an expert on Honduran culture during a post-conviction hearing. Aguirre himself had witnessed three murders growing up: a stabbing at a bus stop when he was fourteen, a man killed by an AK-47 on the soccer field where he routinely played, and the shooting death of his close friend. It was this last killing that was particularly painful, as he had arrived shortly after the shooting and taken his friend in his arms, trying to hold on even as the police had pried his hands free.

And then there were the gangs. Two were prominent in Aguirre's neighborhood when he was growing up: the 18th Street gang where he played soccer, and MS-13 where he lived. By the 1990s, these gangs were so entrenched in Central America's "northern triangle" of Honduras, El Salvador, and Guatemala that the United Nations had declared them responsible for creating the highest homicide rate in the world. A report written for the Department of Justice in 2013 noted that two of the world's most dangerous cities, including Tegucigalpa, where Aguirre had been born, were in Honduras, and that the gangs had "established a reign of terror" there.

In short, it was a good place to leave, and he had tried. As a teenager his mother shipped him off to Nicaragua to live with family, but after a few months he had returned, anxious to finish school in Honduras. When the gangs began recruiting him, though, it was time to leave for good.

But leaving was no easy matter. From Honduras to Guatemala to Nuevo Laredo in Mexico took three months, a new identity, and a phony birth certificate, and he nearly drowned crossing the Rio Grande (known in Mexico as the Rio Bravo, or "fierce river") into Laredo. When he finally entered Texas, he believed he had left the Honduran "reign of terror" behind him. Was he heading north for work and a better life and a sliver of the American dream, or had he washed ashore from the raging river as another illegal immigrant infesting the United States?

This is where the narratives go their separate ways, divorced by perspective and sometimes the facts themselves. For instance, the crime wave of gang violence in the "northern triangle" of Central America had actually originated in Los Angeles, where both gangs formed decades earlier. It was the immigration policy of the United States that had caused the problem in the first place—the deportation of gang members from LA essentially moved the gangs south of the border, where countries with looser criminal enforcement allowed them to flourish. But the circular causation of transnational criminal gangs is just a silent and ironic footnote in today's very loud immigration debate.

Of course, it's not really a debate at all, but a screaming war of words. In much the same way the Bush administration linked the Iraq War to 9/11 by keeping as few syllables between the two topics as possible, the modern anti-immigration Republican narrative repeats three things without taking a breath—American crime, MS-13, and the building of a border wall. But while that storyline has become so familiar over the past few years, it started with the Bush administration as well. As the Aguirre case was winding its way through the courts, Congress passed the Secure Fence Act of 2006 to achieve "operational control" over the Mexican border. The same year the House Committee on Homeland Security issued *A Line in the Sand: Confronting the Threat at the Southwest Border*, noting that "approximately 90 percent of U.S. MS-13 members are foreign-born illegal aliens and depend upon the Texas-Mexico border smuggling corridor to support their criminal operations. MS-13 members are involved in a variety of other types of criminal activity, including rape, murder, and extortion." In short, the immigration die had been cast long before blustering campaign ads over who was paying for a wall. Clemente Aguirre had entered the country illegally, failed to report a gruesome crime, claimed that he lied to the police for fear of being deported, and then was convicted and sentenced to death. Whether he had fled the gangs in Honduras or joined them hardly mattered. He was one of them, and there was no room for debate about what to do with him.

On July 5, 2012, the Aguirre defense attorneys learned more about Samantha Williams than even the drops of her blood at the crime scene had previously revealed. In documents ranging from three years before the murders to six years after, her severe mental health problem manifested itself through four separate interactions with the Seminole County Sheriff's Office. In 2001 she had been committed to the hospital when her mother feared she would hurt herself by banging her head against the wall, which she had been doing since she was eight years old. Although only seventeen, the report indicated that she had been drinking "a lot of beer" and was taking medication for depression. The responding officer noted two "dry bloody cuts" on her forehead—could behavior like this explain how her blood had ended up at the crime scene?

Her next interaction with the sheriff's office was four years after the crime. Very little had changed. The report indicated that she "was out of control, smashing objects in the house, and hurting herself, ramming her head against walls and doors." She was intoxicated and "on medication for being Bipolar." The police felt the need to handcuff her, hobble her feet, and apply a safety belt to make sure she didn't hurt them or herself. A friend of hers was interviewed, stating that "she has been dealing with depression for the last four years, when her Grandmother and Mother were both murdered by a man looking for her." While the police transported her to South Seminole Hospital, she screamed "it's not my fault" and "I want to die" over and over again.

What did she mean—it's not my fault? Clearly she had suffered from severe depression for much of her life, and the violent loss of her mother and grandmother could only add to that. If Clemente Aguirre had been looking for her when he killed the two older women, might she have somehow faulted herself for his actions? Certainly there was plenty of literature to support her feelings. At the same time, though, there was no doubt that she was dangerous—even in restraints, she had threatened to kill the police officers taking her to the hospital, kicked at nurses, and pushed one in the stomach with her foot.

Two years after that, her ambiguous statements took on a much clearer meaning. The fire department had responded to a call of a female who had attempted to set herself on fire; it turned out to be Samantha Williams, and sure enough she was sitting on a comforter that had been burning. A police officer spoke to a neighbor, who reported that Samantha had not been taking her medication and had been saying that demons in her head had caused her to kill her family. And there was one other thing—the police report noted the 2004 case number for the "homicide which occurred in the residence."

It was the date of this report—August 11, 2010—as well as the substance of it that proved to be significant. When Aguirre's attorneys learned of its existence almost two years later, there was an immediate reckoning: the prosecutors had *opposed* further DNA testing after Samantha's blood had been found at the crime scene, and after learning of her statements confessing to the murders. The state's attorney's explanation? "I went on [the state computer system] and did a search looking for something, and I stumbled across these records."

This prompted some back and forth between the defense and the state about how the records had been stored and discovered, but the implication that the state had been hiding information did not bother Judge Recksiedler: "All right. Neither here nor there. Honestly, it doesn't make a difference. The Court's granting the motion . . . and giving [the documents] to [the defense], all right." The judge also agreed with the defense request for further DNA testing, and a few months later that testing revealed six more drops of Samantha Williams's blood within inches of her mother's blood.

Now there were eight drops of blood at the scene of the crime from a woman who had confessed to a friend that she'd killed her mother and grandmother, and no DNA at all from the man who stood convicted of the crime. This seemed like a pretty good time to be asking for a new trial for Clemente Aguirre, and his lawyers did just that. The legal standard was straightforward: if the new evidence weakened the case against the defendant "so as to give rise to a reasonable doubt as to his culpability," he received a new trial.

Given the DNA and the confession by the daughter, maybe Aguirre was telling the truth when he said he had just stopped by and saw the dead bodies? Had he really lied to the police out of fear of deportation rather than guilt? Whatever the reality, it was hard to imagine that the new evidence hadn't created a reasonable doubt about Aguirre's guilt.

Yet that is exactly what Judge Recksiedler found in 2013. In a lengthy and detailed opinion, she held that Samantha's confession was "more in line with expressions of survivor's guilt rather than expressions of guilt in murdering them." Of Samantha's blood found in numerous spots at the crime scene, she said she found it "not compelling"; instead, the judge credited Samantha's "alibi" that she had been with her boyfriend. Indeed, her use of the word *alibi* in the opinion, ordinarily employed in the context of a defendant accused of a crime, seemed to suggest that the judge had unconsciously decided to defend Samantha Williams from conviction, rather than determining whether there was now a reasonable doubt about Clemente Aguirre's guilt.

But the evidence suggesting that Samantha Williams had actually committed the killings soon became even more compelling. Three more people came forward and, under oath, testified that she had confessed to the crime. Two of those witnesses, together at a campsite, had asked Samantha to leave the area, only to be told, "I'm not afraid of you, I killed my mother and my grandmother." Still Judge Recksiedler was unmoved: "Samantha Williams's statements are more likely attempts to frighten individuals who had upset her than true confessions of the crimes." Clemente Aguirre was now spending his eleventh year in custody, and the evidence he hoped would set him free had been declared irrelevant by a judge in Seminole County, Florida.

It is impossible to predict what events will suddenly arise from the unfortunate routine of murder to capture the public's imagination. Perhaps because this crime had taken place in a filthy mobile home in a trailer park, it did not garner much attention: the *Tampa Bay Times* described the case as a "little-known double murder," and the question of Aguirre's innocence a "quiet legal battle." Or perhaps the media were more focused on an incident that did penetrate the nation's consciousness, and had occurred in the same Seminole County at the same time Samantha Williams's DNA and new confessions were coming to light. The killing of Trayvon Martin.

Even before the time of his arrest, the investigation and eventual trial of George Zimmerman was freighted with racial overtones. Captain of his crime watch group, Zimmerman had shot and killed the teenaged Martin after spotting him in Zimmerman's gated community. There were a great many conclusions drawn from the unarmed Martin "looking like he is up to no good," from his wearing a dark hoodie to Zimmerman following him and saying on 911: "these assholes, they always get away." When Zimmerman was released without being charged, the Seminole County law enforcement community came under considerable examination. The subsequent inquiry by a special prosecutor and Zimmerman's acquittal did little to dispel the general aura of racism that pervaded the investigation.

But the Trayvon Martin case was hardly Seminole County's first run-in with allegations of racism. In 1946, one year before breaking the color line in major league baseball, Jackie Robinson had been run out of the county seat of Sanford by the Ku Klux Klan, ultimately requiring his entire minor league team to relocate to Daytona Beach for spring training. On Christmas Day in 1951, the home of the founder of the local branch of the NAACP was firebombed, killing the founder and his wife. Only a year before the Martin killing, the white son of a Sanford police lieutenant had brutally sucker-punched a homeless Black man, prompting allegations of a cover-up and forcing the ouster of the police chief when a video of the incident surfaced and the son wasn't arrested. The town of Sanford itself had been named for a fruit grower named Henry Sanford, who advocated sending Black Americans back to Africa and lobbied Congress on behalf of King Leopold's claim to the Congo as a Belgian colony. It was against this legacy that Clemente Aguirre, a Honduran national convicted of killing two American women, had spent twelve years on death row. The justice system of Seminole County had put him there without a careful look at the evidence, and kept him there after a new suspect had emerged. With a compelling case of innocence in his pocket, Aguirre took his appeal to the Florida Supreme Court.

That court had already ruled against him once; but this time all the evidence that had previously stood in the way of his innocence now began to look like a key to his cell door:

> The importance of the newly discovered evidence is plain when compared with the evidence that the State used to convict Aguirre—i.e., forensic evidence linking Aguirre to the murders and Samantha's testimony . . . [A]dding the newly discovered evidence to the picture changes the focus entirely: No longer is Aguirre the creepy figure who appears over Samantha's bed in the middle of the night; he is now the scapegoat for her crimes. Viewed through this lens, the DNA evidence tending to exculpate Aguirre but inculpate Samantha substantially weakens the case against Aguirre. And when the DNA evidence is considered together with Samantha's numerous, unequivocal confessions, the result is reasonable doubt as to Aguirre's culpability.

Directly reversing every ruling Judge Recksiedler had made, the state's highest court ordered a new trial for Aguirre, practically declaring him innocent. There were only two problems: the trial would take place in Sanford, and the presiding judge would be Recksiedler.

Given the Supreme Court's labeling of Aguirre as a "scapegoat" for the crimes, the prosecution might reasonably have been expected to take a careful look at the evidence before deciding whether to move forward. Almost immediately, however, the state's attorney for Seminole County declared an intention to retry the case; and having doubled down on Clemente Aguirre's guilt, the state determined to seek his death once again. In February 2018 jury selection began; but selecting a jury in Seminole County proved problematic the second time around. A number of the potential jurors had decided to do their own research on the case, and shared the information they had learned:

> Defense Attorney: All right. I would ask you to be forthright with Her Honor as to what it was you said about my client with this case to any other prospective jurors.
> Juror: The only one thing that come [sic] to mind is whether or not he was a citizen of the United States of America.

Why was that important? "That's based on my opinion of what's in the news these days, illegal immigration," the juror said. But it wasn't just that the topic had been in the news: "It's based on the rights of American citizens opposed to an illegal immigrant." In case there was the slightest confusion, he clarified: "And then I carried on with why are we even hearing this case for somebody that's not even a citizen." Another potential juror recalled some of the evidence from the first trial, "and I think I also recall that the defendant is here illegally in the country." A third noted that she overheard some of her fellow jurors saying that "the case was looked up and something about citizenship." But picking a jury wasn't Clemente Aguirre's only problem. The defense team was still dealing with the judge who had casually dismissed Samantha Williams's DNA and confessions.

Judge Recksiedler was no stranger to controversy. In 2015 she had been reprimanded by the chief justice of the Florida Supreme Court for conduct demonstrating "a lack of candor not befitting the high standards of ethical conduct expected of all judges in this state." It seemed the judge was not a safe driver, and had been given at least six traffic tickets for speeding; but the tickets themselves had not gotten her reprimanded. When she went before a panel interviewing her for a job as an appeals court judge, she acknowledged to its members that they might be concerned with her driving record. What she didn't acknowledge was that she had gotten a speeding ticket on the very morning she had driven to her interview. It was that silence the chief justice had labeled "an ethical violation." But her driving record was not of paramount concern to Aguirre's lawyers; more pressing was what they felt was her continuing misconduct in the Aguirre case itself.

In late December 2016, after the state Supreme Court had reversed her opinion and ordered a new trial, she had conducted a hearing on the case without the presence of a court reporter or Aguirre, violating clear rules of the Florida courts. Two months later the defense learned that Recksiedler had allowed her state-mandated accreditation for the handling of death penalty cases to lapse, apparently not anticipating the possibility of a new trial despite her opinion to the contrary. But none of those gaffes caused the consternation that occurred after seven brutally long days of jury selection. First, without consultation from the prosecution or the defense, and then over objections from each side, the judge dismissed the entire panel of possible jurors. Perhaps she was being excessively cautious to safeguard a fair trial for Aguirre; but a more disturbing motive emerged when the judge insisted that jury selection would pick back up one month later, even after the lawyers advised her that they would be unavailable.

Two weeks before the next trial date, the defense filed a lengthy motion asking Recksiedler to recuse herself from the case. Aside from a detailed list of judicial mistakes (such as three times announcing that Aguirre had pleaded guilty to the charges), the defense revealed a shocking claim: Recksiedler had tried to rush the trial to completion, and when she realized it might not be finished in time, had dismissed the potential jury and then immediately rescheduled the case, all to ensure that she wouldn't miss a family vacation. Producing evidence that her publicly available docket indicated "NO COURT" from March 16 to 23, that the Seminole County public schools were closed for those dates, and that the defense had "information and belief that Judge Recksiedler has a family vacation planned for the week of March 19," the attorneys made the following claim:

> Whether the Court was influenced by its civil docket or personal calendar, Mr. Aguirre has a well-founded and reasonable concern that, in light of these facts, the Court is inclined to prioritize its calendar over his constitutional rights, or is unable (or unwilling) to sufficiently plan for contingencies that would protect both.

Six days after these allegations were formally filed, Judge Recksiedler wrote that "perceptions, however ill-conceived in this matter, could distract the State and/or the Defense from performing their necessary functions." She then recused herself from any further participation in the case.

*   *   *

Death penalty lawyers like to talk about "changing the picture." By this they mean that the prosecution will inevitably present a harsh, devastating, and often monstrous vision of the crime and the accused, and it is the job of the defense to craft a more nuanced and human presentation. Clemente Aguirre's second trial already had a very different explanation for the physical evidence, and clearly another suspect had emerged. But the defense investigation continued, and it focused on Samantha Williams's "alibi," her boyfriend Mark Van Sandt.

While the new evidence profoundly changed the picture of the crime, time had clarified some of the old evidence as well. For starters, Van Sandt had been in and out of jail a number of times since the first trial, and his many recorded conversations on prison phones left the impression less of a dutiful boyfriend and more of a swindler trying to get out from under his own problems. He had told his wife, Nicole, and his mother that he was testifying in return for a deal from the prosecution to get out of jail, a claim the prosecution adamantly denied. But as Nicole related under oath in an affidavit just before the beginning of the second trial, Mark Van Sandt was even more of a liar than the phone records indicated:

> Mark . . . told me that Samantha had suffered a single stab wound that night in the attack and that she had also died that night. He did not say that he had seen Samantha's body, but that she had been found by the police . . . Later . . . Mark told me for the first time that Samantha had told him that she killed her mother and grandmother . . . I came to learn that Samantha Williams was in fact alive and had not died in the attack on her mother and grandmother. This came as a shock to me because

Mark had told me that Samantha died the same night as her mother and grandmother. I could not understand why Mark would have lied to me about such a thing.

There was more. Van Sandt had testified at the first trial that Samantha and he had slept through the night of the crime, thus inoculating her from any wrongdoing. But Nicole's affidavit told a very different story: "Mark has consistently told me that Samantha Williams woke him up during the night of June 16–17, 2004, said she 'had a bad feeling about her mom,' and left through the window of his bedroom. Mark has made these statements to me both before and after we were married." The final straw might have been on Halloween, when Mark Van Sandt testified in a deposition about the many lies he had told to his wife and others:

Q (by defense counsel): So let me ask you again: are you
    a pathological liar; yes or no?
A: I've had problems with the truth before; yes.
Q: So yes. You are a pathological liar.
A: I—I can't diagnose myself.
Q: But you think that that's a potential diagnosis for you;
    don't you?
A: Could be.

This was more than just a changing of the picture—the new suspect in the double killing had just lost her "alibi," and the prosecution had lost any chance of convicting Clemente Aguirre. As Hemingway said in a different context, the prosecution's case had collapsed gradually, then suddenly.

On November 5, 2018, the lead trial attorney for the state walked into the Seminole County Criminal Justice Center and announced that all charges were being dropped. In a public statement released the same day, the state's attorney demonstrated the sort of cognitive dissonance that comes with the recognition that you've had the wrong man on death row while the right woman went free: "While the State has serious concerns about the credibility of Mr. Aguirre-Jarquin's statement of facts regarding his participation in this incident, the State does not believe further incarceration of Mr. Aguirre-Jarquin is warranted or justified at this time."

Yet further incarceration was still a possibility. Three days before the dismissal, and more than fourteen years after his imprisonment, the Department of Homeland Security had placed an immigration hold on him. Only after an immigration judge allowed him bail did he finally walk out of custody a free man. "It's harder to get out than to get in," he said only moments after his release. "I can guarantee you that."

Almost three years later Clemente Aguirre remains in Florida awaiting removal proceedings. He has a number of options, including asylum based on the past and present conditions in Honduras, and perhaps status as a lawful permanent resident based on being the victim of a crime. This second option, otherwise known as a U visa, "is set aside for victims of certain crimes who have suffered mental or physical abuse and are helpful to law enforcement or government officials in the investigation or prosecution of criminal activity." Perjury is one of the "qualifying criminal activities," according to the official website of the Department of Homeland Security, and surely the perjury of Samantha Williams and Mark Van Sandt that landed him on death row would meet that criteria. But there is a catch, familiar to anyone who does "innocence work" in the criminal justice system: law enforcement officials are often the last people to admit they made a mistake, and in Aguirre's case, not a single law enforcement agency has been willing to come forward to validate his innocence. A bill to compensate him for "being wrongfully incarcerated for nearly 15 years" was introduced in the Florida House of Representatives, but it died in committee just as the pandemic exploded in March 2020. His lawyers have filed a parallel lawsuit seeking damages for the state's failure to "adequately investigate" the crime, and that complaint has survived most of the challenges by law enforcement. In short, he may yet be financially compensated for his lost years. However, as the federal judge overseeing the lawsuit noted: "Some losses, like liberty, can't ever be repaid and some wrongs can't ever be made truly right."

Will he be allowed to remain in this country? Considerable discretion is built into immigration decisions, and certainly spending more than a decade on Florida's death row for the crime of an American citizen will weigh in his favor. The 1790 Naturalization Act, while limiting immigration to "free white persons," also introduced the concept of an applicant's good moral character, an issue that has been pondered since Plato but given short shrift in today's dialogue about the country's borders. Clemente Aguirre's first moments of freedom might have provided an answer. "What do you have to say to Samantha Williams," Clemente Aguirre was asked in the Immigration and Customs Enforcement parking lot. There was a lengthy pause. "I forgive you," he said.

11

The N-Word in the Jury Box

On April 12, 2005, almost eight years after Kenneth Fults went to death row for kidnapping and killing his neighbor Cathy Bounds in Spalding County, Georgia, Thomas Buffington declared under oath that the death penalty was "what that [n-word] deserved." Fults was a Black man, and Bounds was a white woman, and it is hardly shocking that some people might have harbored racist thoughts under such charged circumstances, particularly since Fults had pled guilty to the crime. Buffington's statement, while unfortunate, would not have been newsworthy at all but for one fact—he was a juror who decided Fults should be executed.

Nine years later, after every lower court had denied Fults's claim that he'd been sentenced by a biased juror, a federal appeals court joined the chorus when it refused to consider how racism might have affected his trial and sentencing. It was his last real opportunity to receive justice from an unbiased jury.

Such refusals are not nearly as surprising as they may sound. State and federal courts across the country have routinely avoided the evidence and consequences of racism in the criminal justice system. Perhaps the most famous example is the

1987 U.S. Supreme Court case of *McCleskey v. Kemp*. Lawyers for death row inmate Warren McCleskey, a Black man who had killed a white police officer, offered statistical research from more than two thousand Georgia murder cases that established a very clear racial bias against Black defendants who kill white victims. The numbers, even thirty-four years later, are shocking: while 1 percent of the cases involving Black defendants and Black victims resulted in a death sentence, 22 percent involving a Black defendant and a white victim did. Nor did the bias show itself only in jury sentences—prosecutors sought death in 70 percent of murders involving Black defendants and white victims but only 15 percent of those involving Black defendants and Black victims.

Yet such compelling data failed to move the Supreme Court. Speaking for a 5–4 majority, Justice Lewis Powell, in an opinion he later called his greatest regret on the bench, wrote that McCleskey's claim could not prevail because the evidence did not establish that "the decision-makers in *his* case acted with discriminatory purpose." Toward the end of the decision, Powell finally got to his real concern: "McCleskey's claim, taken to its logical conclusion, throws into serious question the principles that underlie our entire criminal justice system."

Justice William Brennan, nearing the end of an iconic career on the Court, responded with perhaps the most memorable phrase of his 1,360 opinions. Noting that the majority's unwillingness to consider McCleskey's claim was based in part on its concern that it would open the door to pervasive challenges to all aspects of criminal sentencing, he wrote: "Taken on its face, such a statement seems to suggest a fear of too much justice." He went on: "The prospect that there may be more widespread abuse than McCleskey documents may be dismaying, but it does not justify complete abdication of our judicial role." Complete abdication or not, McCleskey was executed by the state of Georgia in 1991.

The *McCleskey* rationale—what the *New York Times* labeled the "impossible burden" of proving that racial animus specifically motivated the prosecutor, judge, or jury of the accused—has been used by dozens of courts to reject statistical claims of discrimination in capital cases. But Kenneth Fults was not trying to circumvent *McCleskey* with a complex regression analysis that established a pattern of bias—rather, he was presenting an actual juror in his own case explaining his decision to impose the death penalty through the lens of his own vile racism. In other words, Fults was introducing exactly the sort of evidence *McCleskey* required, that a decision-maker in his case acted with discriminatory purpose. Which led to two obvious questions: How did Thomas Buffington manage to sit on Kenneth Fults's jury in the first place, and how did the courts manage to ignore the evidence of Buffington's racism?

Justice Powell's concerns are understandable. After all, what part of the criminal justice system is untouched by racism? Some death penalty critics, in fact, view capital punishment as a direct descendent of lynching. The phrase *legal lynching* first appeared in the *New York Times* during the infamous 1931 Scottsboro Boys trials, in which nine Black youths were charged with raping two white women in Alabama. Their lack of counsel, coupled with the explicit exclusion of Black jurors, led the Supreme Court to intercede twice and reverse convictions.

It's hard to read those opinions today without feeling a sense of horror: within two weeks of the alleged crime, eight of the nine men had been sentenced to death in three separate trials by the same jury. Although more than 7 percent of Scottsboro

County's population was comprised of Black men eligible to serve on juries, there was no record of any of them ever serving on one. Perhaps most remarkably, none of the defendants had a lawyer appointed to represent him until the morning of trial. In 2013, more than eighty years after the arrests, the Alabama Board of Pardons and Paroles posthumously pardoned the three Scottsboro Boys whose convictions still stood.

We have not come nearly as far from these outrages as you might think. People of color are still dramatically underrepresented on juries and grand juries, even though excluding people based on race is illegal and undermines "public confidence in our system of justice," as the Supreme Court put it in 1986. Prospective Black jurors are routinely dismissed at higher rates than whites. The law simply requires some rationale other than skin color.

"Question them at length," a prominent Philadelphia prosecutor suggested to his protégés after the Supreme Court banned race as a reason for striking jurors. "Mark something down that you can articulate at a later time." For instance, "Well, the woman had a kid about the same age as the defendant and I thought she'd be sympathetic to him."

In 2005, a former prosecutor in Texas said that she'd been instructed by her superiors to falsely claim that a Black prospective juror had been sleeping if she wanted to get him out of the jury pool. This was just a dressed-up version of the Dallas prosecution training manual from 1963, which directed assistant district attorneys to "not take Jews, Negroes, Dagos, Mexicans, or a member of any minority race on a jury, no matter how rich or how well educated." The 1969 edition of the manual, which was used into the 1980s, had been updated to recommend more subtle stereotyping: It was "not advisable to select potential jurors with multiple gold chains around their necks." But it hardly mattered: overt, covert, or in between—the result was the same.

Virtually every state with a death penalty has dealt with accusations that Black jurors have been improperly kept off juries. During the 1992 death penalty trial of a defendant named George Williams, a California prosecutor dismissed the first five Black women in the jury box, explaining that "sometimes you get a feel for a person that you just know that they can't impose it based upon the nature of the way that they say something." The judge went even further, noting that "black women are very reluctant to impose the death penalty; they find it very difficult." In 2013, the state Supreme Court ruled that those jury strikes were not race-based, and deemed the judge's statement "isolated." Williams remains on death row.

After North Carolina passed the Racial Justice Act, a 2009 law that let inmates challenge their death sentences based on racial bias, a state court determined that prosecutors were dismissing Black jurors at twice the rate of other jurors. The probability of this being a race-neutral fluke, according to two professors from Michigan State University, was less than one in ten trillion; even the state's expert agreed that the disparity was statistically significant. Based on these numbers, the court vacated the death sentences of three inmates, resentencing each to life without parole. Six months later, the legislature repealed the Racial Justice Act.

But the North Carolina story didn't end there. In August 2020, the newly progressive North Carolina Supreme Court ruled that the repeal was not retroactive, and in so doing removed Marcus Robinson from death row. The opinion pointed out that prosecutors had been trained in 1995 and 2011 how to circumvent constitutional requirements of jury selection, and highlighted handwritten notes made by a prosecutor in a different capital case: an African American juror with a criminal history was called a "thug," while a white juror with a criminal record was a "fine guy." An African American juror was a "blk wino," while a white juror with a conviction for driving while impaired was a "country boy—ok."

So how did Thomas Buffington end up on Fults's jury in the first place? The answer is simple: he lied. Here's the relevant snippet from jury selection:

> Defense Attorney: Do you have any racial prejudice resting on your mind?
> Buffington: No, sir.
> Defense Attorney: Does it make any difference that in this case the defendant is Black and the victim was white?
> Buffington: No, sir.

Even this sort of cursory questioning wasn't required by the Supreme Court until 1986, and then only in capital cases—and when the defense requests it. In order to function, the justice system has to presume that jurors will tell the truth under oath, just as it presumes lawyers are competent.

And what of the lawyer's role? Since 1976, when mandatory death sentences were ruled unconstitutional, the decision of whether to seek execution has rested entirely with the local district attorney. In practice, this means a white man usually gets to decide who should face the death chamber. A 2015 study found that 95 percent of elected prosecutors in the United States were white, and the overwhelming majority were male.

In the Fults case, that white man was William McBroom, district attorney of the Griffin Judicial Circuit. McBroom had already put two men on death row by the time he prosecuted

Fults, and continued to aggressively seek and obtain death verdicts until 2004, when he lost his reelection by a hair. He wasn't the type to fret over moral ambiguities: McBroom sought death sentences at every opportunity, thereby avoiding allegations of discrimination in the charging process.

McBroom's tough approach found an unlikely ally in Johnny B. Mostiler, the Spalding County public defender, who happened to be representing Kenneth Fults. "We're finding ourselves facing crimes we think are Atlanta big-city crimes," Mostiler said at one point. "We're a law-abiding town. We want our criminals prosecuted."

McBroom and Mostiler knew each other so well that the Fults transcript sometimes reads like old friends reminiscing: McBroom points out how Mostiler is going to respond, mentions an argument his rival made in an earlier case, and refers to him by his first name before handing over the floor for closing arguments. "Mostiler was the toughest trial lawyer in Spalding County," McBroom recalled some years after the Fults trial. "He would take cases where you didn't think defendants had a chance, and you'd be fighting for your life."

But of course McBroom had every reason to praise Mostiler: a death verdict is invariably followed by appeals in which the defense attorney's work comes under close scrutiny. Prosecutors routinely hail their adversaries as giants in the field of capital defense to make it harder for any defendant to later claim his lawyer was incompetent. And McBroom, who had obtained death verdicts against Mostiler in several prior cases, needed to defend some deplorable behavior. For all intents and purposes, Johnny Mostiler, like Thomas Buffington, was a racist.

Spalding County, forty miles south of Atlanta, had but a single public defender to represent criminal defendants who couldn't afford an attorney—and a great majority could not. All through the 1990s, Mostiler was that defender, responsible for handling as many as nine hundred felonies a year. He also maintained a significant civil practice on the side and took on serious felony cases outside of Spalding County. But he was hardly your humble, nose-to-the-grindstone type. According to a 2001 profile in the *American Prospect,* Mostiler stood out in a black cowboy hat; a silver beard with handlebar mustache; six gold, silver, and onyx rings; and three gold bracelets. He drove a mustard-green 1972 Cadillac El Dorado convertible with cattle horns as a hood ornament.

But Mostiler's true legacy—he died of a heart attack a few years after the Fults trial—would involve the case of Curtis Osborne, a former client tried by McBroom in 1991, found guilty of murder, and scheduled for execution in 2008. As the clock wound down on his appeals, a former U.S. attorney general, a former Georgia chief justice, and former president Jimmy Carter, previously the governor of Georgia, spoke out against the execution. They had all heard the allegation by another of Mostiler's clients, a white man named Gerald Huey, that Mostiler had told him "that little [n-word] deserves the chair."

Some time after that, a Georgia lawyer named Arleen Evans stepped forward with a sworn recollection about Mostiler:

> I recall one occasion when I was in the lawyer's lounge at the Spalding County Courthouse. There were a number of other lawyers there including Mr. Mostiler. Mr. Mostiler began telling racist jokes filled with racial epithets like "[n-word]." Some of the lawyers would laugh. Some would laugh nervously. Some would try to ignore it. And others would leave the room to get away from it. On another occasion, I remember walking into the lawyer's lounge and Mr. Mostiler was again telling racist jokes. Ms. Nancy Bradford, who is now deceased, looked at me,

noticed that it was making me uncomfortable, and told me "that's just Johnny."

Osborne's lawyers soon dug up more evidence: a transcript from the trial of Derrick Middlebrooks, a Black defendant so troubled by Mostiler's racist talk that he asked the judge to dismiss Mostiler as his public defender: "He indicated to me that he wouldn't—he couldn't go up there among them [n-words] because them [n-words] would kill him," Middlebrooks said. "Now personally I don't know if he meant anything really by it. But I find it, you know, kind of hard to have an attorney to represent me when he uses those type of words. It doesn't help my confidence in my attorney."

"I honestly don't remember," Mostiler responded when the judge questioned him about it. "I don't use those terms out in public. And I probably—if I did use it I certainly am sorry. I didn't mean to indicate that it was any—or any racial overtones. I think my—I think my record on race is . . ."

"Well documented in this court," the judge interjected.

Mostiler was long dead by the time his racist language became an issue in the *Osborne* case, but several prosecutors, including McBroom and his successor, District Attorney Scott Ballard, spoke up on his behalf. Mostiler had presented a "very adequate defense" of Curtis Osborne, Ballard argued. He urged that the execution go forward.

Small counties tend to have incestuous legal communities. Public defenders and assistant district attorneys often swap sides and socialize together, too; top assistants become bosses, and, most predictably, district attorneys end up on the bench.

Such was the case with Fults's trial judge, Johnnie Caldwell, who preceded McBroom as DA of the Griffin Judicial Circuit. As both county prosecutor and judge, Caldwell was well aware of the racism allegations surrounding Mostiler. It was Cald-well, in fact, who heard Middlebrooks's claims and used the opportunity to assure Mostiler, saying: "It's unchallenged in this court with your actions concerning the races and certainly of standing up for the rights of all individuals regardless of their race or color or religious preference." Turning to Middle-brooks, Caldwell added: "I find nothing in Mr. Mostiler's con-duct of this trial or in representing you that would cause me to disqualify him."

By suggesting that the public defender of Spal-ding County—a man hired year after year by the county commissioners—was a racist, Middlebrooks had also, unwit-tingly, impugned the dignity of the prosecutor and the presid-ing judge. Caldwell was clearly put out:

> Middlebrooks: My motion for a new attorney is denied?
> Caldwell: Yes, sir.
> Middlebrooks: Okay. Thank you.
> Caldwell: And I know you're sitting over there reading a book on ineffective assistance of counsel, you read it real well and write everything down, okay.
> Middlebrooks: Yes, sir.
> Caldwell: I'm directing you to. You write everything down and you write it well. You've been reading that book ever since you've been sitting over there.
> Middlebrooks: Judge, that has—
> Caldwell: Sir, don't say anything else.
> Middlebrooks: Yes, sir.

When race became an issue in the Osborne case, Caldwell didn't step forward to disclose his interactions with Mostiler, nor did any of those other lawyers in the lounge, who had no doubt heard the same racist jokes and comments Arleen Evans had. (Caldwell had his own problems, in any case. He resigned his judgeship in 2010 in light of allegations that he was soliciting female attorneys in open court. He was nonetheless elected, not long after, to the Georgia legislature, and served until 2019.)

Ultimately, neither the local nor federal courts were moved by the consistency of the testimony concerning Mostiler's racist talk. In 2006, the Eleventh Circuit Court of Appeals soundly rejected Osborne's claim that Mostiler was ineffective counsel due to his racial animosity. Osborne was executed two years later. Citing *McCleskey*, the court said it was the racial animus of the decision-makers—the prosecutors and the jurors, not the defense attorney—that mattered. So what would the same court say eight years later, when lawyers for Kenneth Fults came before it with claims of racial animus involving a decision-maker, the juror Thomas Buffington?

In September 2013, a three-judge panel of the Eleventh Circuit Court of Appeals convened in Miami to hear Fults's claim. Half of their questions focused on technical legal hurdles, such as procedural default, cause and prejudice, impeachment of the verdict, and waiver. The other half dealt with the inexcusable nature of Buffington's admission. The state wanted the court to reject Fults's bias claim by arguing a violation of the rules of evidence, and Adalberto Jordan, the most outspoken of the judges, was struggling to understand why. "When you have a claim of a juror potentially recommending a sentence of death because of flat out racial bias," Jordan asked, "why would the state of Georgia not want that claim heard on the merits?"

Assistant Attorney General Sabrina Graham insisted that

Georgia law was clear on the issue: a verdict could not be reversed based on jury deliberations, no matter what any juror had to say about them afterward. In the process, she spent some awkward moments trying to persuade Jordan and Judge Stanley Marcus that what Buffington said wasn't as damning as it sounded.

Graham: I think there could not be any prejudice.

Marcus: Tell me why there wouldn't be prejudice, if in fact the juror was tainted with racism that affected his decision-making process? . . .

Graham: I don't think you would have enough information to show that. Certainly Mr. Buffington uses a racially derogatory term. I do not think that his particular affidavit shows that he sentenced Mr. Fults to death based upon his racism. People have many prejudices . . .

Jordan: "I knew I would vote for the death penalty because that's what that [n-word] deserved." You want something more specific than that?

Graham: I think you do want something more specific.

Jordan: Like?

Graham: That was eight years after . . .

Jordan: Like? Like what?

Graham: Like I sentenced him to death based upon his race . . .

Marcus: Let's suppose, just to take this to its logical conclusion, that there were 12 affidavits from all 12 jurors who voted for death, and each and every one of them said the same thing . . . Even if every juror says, "I voted to execute him because he was black," you say "That's the law?"

Graham: That is the law.

That's when Jordan, seemingly surprised by Graham's answer, suggested that there was a "safety valve under Georgia law." That is, if an evidentiary rule resulted in a violation of a defendant's constitutional rights, it might justify an exception to that rule.

Graham conceded that such a ruling might be possible: "They have left that possibility open, but they have never actually done anything about it." She then pointed out that there are many reasons to trust a juror's answers during jury selection rather than statements the juror might make after a verdict of death is returned: "Fine, you want to say Mr. Buffington lied during voir dire. [But] you have the trial court, and you have defense counsel all watching these jurors."

Graham was suggesting, in essence, that Johnny Mostiler, who had been accused of racism more than once, and Judge Caldwell, who'd belittled the claim of racism against Mostiler before being removed from the bench for harassing women in his own court, were suitable watchdogs to ensure an impartial jury. Was it possible she didn't realize who they were?

The Eleventh Circuit was not entirely unfamiliar with juror bias. Back in 1986, a man named Daniel Neal Heller had been convicted of tax evasion in Florida. Evidence showed that Heller, a Jewish man, was the butt of anti-Semitic jokes in the jury room that consistently prompted "gales of laughter." The trial judge, when confronted by vague claims of discriminatory comments by the jury, cursorily asked each juror if he or she was "affected by prejudice." The Eleventh Circuit's three-judge panel reversed Heller's conviction, writing that the jurors' religious prejudice was "shocking to the conscience," and concluding: "The people cannot be expected to respect their judicial system if its judges do not, first, do so."

The Eleventh Circuit judges hearing the *Fults* case seemed

to have forgotten the lessons of *Heller*. Despite their pointed questioning during oral arguments, the opinion they released less than a year later expressed neither shocked consciences nor fear of diminished respect for the system. If they were offended by Buffington's admission, it was lost amid all of the procedural arcana.

The prevailing narrative about legal technicalities, thanks to Hollywood portrayals and posturing politicians, is that they open jailhouse doors—which is one reason crime sometimes seems to be on the rise when in fact it is plummeting. In reality, though, legal technicalities are far more often used to preclude people from having their post-conviction claims heard. The *Fults* opinion, written by the outspoken Judge Jordan, is a virtual primer on how the law has evolved to block, rather than illuminate, allegations of injustice.

During oral arguments, Jordan seemed to be advocating for a hearing to determine the circumstances of Buffington's admission. In his opinion, however, he condemned the defense for failing to provide sufficient detail about how or when Buffington's prejudice was discovered. While he had earlier questioned why Georgia didn't want a claim of "flat out racial bias" heard on its merits, his opinion articulated every reason the claim had not been properly presented, and now could not be considered.

Finally, "in an abundance of caution," he addressed the argument he seemed to be championing eleven months earlier: that the failure to consider Fults's prejudice claim would be a miscarriage of justice. Once again he felt compelled to explain that this claim had not been properly presented. Nonetheless, Jordan concluded that Fults failed to show that his sentence was a miscarriage of justice. For while it's true that in Georgia a single juror can stop a death sentence from being imposed— the jury must be unanimous—the bar is much higher for a death row inmate to overturn his sentence. Fults's legal burden was to demonstrate that no reasonable juror would have voted to give him the death penalty. And this, in the court's view, he had not done.

So how, exactly, does a "reasonable juror" think? It's difficult to conceive of any decision more subjective than who should live or die. Every death penalty state has a statute with language intended to objectify the determination, but when all is said and done, it's highly personal: Will the person be a danger in the future? Do the circumstances of the crime overshadow the defendant's background? Do the reasons for a life sentence outweigh those for a death sentence?

And how might this hypothetical reasonable juror regard Kenneth Fults? The man pleaded guilty to a horrible crime. He committed two burglaries and stole some handguns, all with the intention of killing a man involved with his former girlfriend. Instead, he ended up shooting a neighbor, Cathy Bounds, five times in the back of the head.

But, as the Supreme Court points out, there are "potentially infinite" reasons a juror might want to sentence someone who has committed a heinous crime to something other than death. Kenneth Fults's history was packed with them. "I just lost sight of raising my kids," his mother, Juanita Fults, told a state court judge, explaining the result of her crack and alcohol addictions. She was court-martialed from the military for writing bad checks to buy drugs, moved her children from house to house and state to state, abused them with switches and belts and electrical cords—using the plug end when the cord itself ceased to have the necessary impact. Whatever boyfriend happened to be with her at the time often joined in. As for Kenneth's father, the man was no more than a name to him.

Juanita Fults didn't just lose sight of raising her children—she lost sight of them entirely. Kenneth's younger sister remembered how she abandoned the kids after moving the family to Houston:

> We stayed there alone without any adults watching over us so long that the power company had turned off all the utilities. We didn't have heat or lights; I don't remember if we had water. I don't remember how long we were alone . . . I know it was at least a couple of months. I was really scared. Kenny and Michael tried to make it like it was fun and we were just camping out or something. I know they started stealing for us to have something to eat, because we did not have any money. I also remember that Michael had them dig a hole in the ground in the backyard to bury some of our food to try and keep it cold when our electricity was turned off.

But the most compelling legal reason not to sentence Fults to death was that he might have been intellectually disabled. Three separate IQ tests over a sixteen-year period, one of them seven years prior to the murder, all fell within the range for intellectual disability. By seventh grade, Fults was testing near the bottom in basic skills. In eighth, he was placed in a "special class . . . for slow learners"; in that class, a former teacher recalled, Kenny was the "poorest performing student." There was abundant testimony that he was incapable of keeping his money straight or filling out job applications. And growing up, he was most comfortable with far younger children.

Even Judge Jordan, in rejecting Fults's claim of intellectual disability in the Eleventh Circuit, acknowledged that his lawyers' argument was "not without some force." But again, procedural rules came into play: since the state court had rejected the claim, its decision was presumed correct, and only "clear and convincing" evidence could overturn it. The IQ tests, the academic struggles, the affidavits of family members and teachers and friends detailing his "slowness"—none of that was enough. As for what a reasonable juror might have done with all of this information, we'll never know. Johnny Mostiler didn't present any of it to the jury.

Kenneth Fults had one last stop before his appeals ran out. The likelihood that the U.S. Supreme Court will review any matter is remote, but there was a tiny sliver of hope for him in a civil case, *Warger v. Shauers*, that the Court had decided in December 2014. On its face, the unanimous ruling was to Fults's detriment: Justice Sonia Sotomayor's majority opinion echoes what lawyer Sabrina Graham had argued on Georgia's behalf in the Fults case: that what a juror says later cannot be used to attack the verdict.

But in the fine print of that opinion was a footnote that might have been Fults's saving grace: "There may be cases of juror bias so extreme that, almost by definition, the jury trial right has been abridged. If and when such a case arises, the Court can consider whether the usual safeguards are or are not sufficient to protect the integrity of the process."

It was not to be. The Supreme Court failed to step in, and Kenneth Fults was executed on April 12, 2016. Although he had visited with seventeen relatives earlier in the day, he was alone in the execution chamber. The only word he spoke was in response to the chaplain's prayer: *Amen.*

How do we know when we've crossed the line, when our system of justice simply can't tolerate a result that our technical rules encourage? Here's Buffington's full statement: "That [n-word] got just what should have happened. Once he pled guilty, I knew I would vote for the death penalty because that's what that [n-word] deserved."

Racism doesn't get much clearer than that, but it was not enough to save Kenneth Fults. Instead his execution stands for the procedural barriers erected to avoid what Justice Brennan called the fear of too much justice. Our ability to overcome that fear in the future will determine the direction of our criminal justice system.

12

Smoke

For Maggie, in Memory

One thing was for sure and two things were for certain: I could not represent Rafiq Fields if I didn't understand that he had nothing to do with the double murder outside the Red Rock Lounge in northwest Philly. Not claim that he was innocent, not act as if he were innocent, not litigate to show his innocence—*understand that he was innocent*. If I could do this, if I could put aside all the lawyer crap I had learned over the years, all the tricks and deceptions, then I could represent Rafiq Fields. He made it sound like an honor.

So we started out with a big problem, because death penalty lawyers have a regrettable but understandable tendency to consider innocence the defense of last resort. We know that a failed innocence claim is the most likely path to a death sentence—not only has the accused exhibited a lack of remorse, but he has had the unmitigated gall to try to trick the jury. No decent defense attorney starts out with an *understanding* that his client is innocent, or any understanding at all, for that matter. When it comes to the question of innocence or guilt, you learn the evidence, you scrutinize the evidence, you challenge the evidence, you might even be fortunate enough to suppress the evidence, but it is always about *the evidence*. I didn't say any of this to Rafiq Fields, however. Instead I said, "I do understand." But I could tell he didn't believe me. "One thing's for sure, two things are for certain," he said. "You ain't getting me to plead to this, I don't care if they offer probation." I had not even mentioned the possibility of a plea, and probation for a double murder was an urban myth, but I nodded knowingly. This was the end of the beginning of my relationship with Rafiq Fields.

The Crime

The Red Rock Lounge was plainly visible from the regional rail line connecting Chestnut Hill with downtown Philadelphia. As I lived just outside Chestnut Hill, I got to view the crime scene twice a day. According to the police reports the location was a confusion of ballistics and blood—an argument started outside the Lounge, a crowd gathered, shots were fired, and two men were dead. One victim, John Jackson, died instantly; his body was on the sidewalk directly in front of the bar when the police arrived within minutes of the shooting. The second victim, Lyle Tyson, had staggered down the street and around the corner, where he lay choking in his own blood when the police found him.

"Help me, help me, I'm dying," Tyson said.

"Who shot you?" asked Officer Holland.

"Smoke," Tyson whispered.

"Smoke like from a fire?"

"Yes."

They loaded him into an ambulance and took him to Albert Einstein Medical Center, where he was pronounced dead forty-five minutes later.

Eight witnesses were interviewed by the police. Three names of interest emerged: Arnold Newcombe, Victor Byrd, and Jake. Most of the witnesses identified Newcombe as "running" the bar, not in the sense of managing the Lounge but more in charge of all illegal rackets in the general area, mostly drugs and gambling. Byrd was noted by almost everyone as an eyewitness, and had told several people that Jake was the shooter—but Byrd himself had never been interviewed by the police. Several witnesses stated they had heard that Jake did the shooting, but no one claimed to have actually seen him do it. Five witnesses identified a man named Smokes as a participant in the argument, and two of them noted that Rafiq Fields's nickname was Smokes. Another witness saw Rafiq walking up the street after the shooting with a gun in his hand. Arnold Newcombe, the man in charge, identified Rafiq Fields as the shooter.

Two weeks later the police interviewed three more people. Since "Jake" was mentioned as a possible shooter, the police rounded up the usual Jakes and found two. Jake Long said that he lived near the Lounge, but that he was on a religious retreat in the Poconos on the night in question. Jake Powers stated that he was in fact at the Red Rock celebrating his birthday, but that he left around midnight, a good two hours before the shooting. The last witness, Rashon Howell, had recently been arrested for a car theft, and the police spoke to him in jail. He told them that he watched the shooting through the window of the bar, and that Rafiq Fields shot both men, then stepped over the man who fell and punched him in the face. This last fact was consistent with the medical examiner's report detailing a fractured right orbital on the face of John Jackson that was inconsistent with a terminal fall.

The homicide detectives considered what they had—two witnesses identified Rafiq Fields as the shooter. Maybe they weren't the cleanest of citizens, but homicide witnesses rarely were. Besides, they were corroborated by the broken eye of one of the victims, which supported the account of Rashon Howell, and a third witness who saw Fields walking down the street after the shooting with a gun. Not to mention the coup de grace—victim Tyson's dying declaration that Smoke, aka Rafiq Fields, had shot him. Yes, there was some hearsay about a man named Jake, and an alleged eyewitness named Byrd who apparently didn't want to be found; but when all was said and done the police trod the predictable path and arrested Fields for the murders of Jackson and Tyson. After all, no case was perfect, but this one was considerably better than most.

The Team

Capital defense is not solitary work. To do it correctly requires a team of investigators, assorted experts, and, most crucially, mitigation specialists; ours was Dana Cook. I left out the law-yers, of which you need at least two. Often that last part is the catch, and what separates the craft of criminal defense from the art of capital defense. Criminal lawyers don't grow up as team players, and forcing them to listen to any voice but their own is often like making children share their favorite toys. But a death penalty case, like any complex litigation, is too much work for one, so every death penalty lawyer has a partner; and this partnership can last the length of a case, or as long as the two can stand to work with each other. My partner, for seventeen years, was Karl Schwartz; but Rafiq Fields came as close as any client ever did to ending this remarkable associ-ation. And ultimately, the challenge of the team was three-pronged: not to let the state kill Rafiq Fields; not to kill him ourselves; and not to let him provoke us into killing each other.

The Investigation

Many cases are won in court. Good cross-examination and a powerful closing argument can often persuade a jury, and these skills are the stock in trade of the successful defense attorney, who makes a living questioning the credibility of biased police officers, confused eyewitnesses, and hapless victims. But capital cases are not won in court—the crimes are too heinous, the victims too devastated. Such cases are so terrible that capital litigators often redefine the notion of victory to include anything less than the death of their client.

Capital cases are won in investigation. Not the thrilling investigation of dark movies and late-night car chases, but the labor-intensive and occasionally stultifying gathering of documents and speaking to all sorts of witnesses, not just of the crime but also of the background of the client. It was this sort of investigation that we began in the Fields case, and our starting point was Victor Byrd.

Byrd, you may recall, was the reluctant eyewitness. It is not unusual for eyewitnesses to be reluctant; indeed, it is unusual when they are not. But Byrd separated himself from the typical in three significant ways: (1) instead of simply lying to the police and saying he had seen nothing, he took the rare step of fleeing; (2) instead of ducking out to his mother's house in North Philadelphia, where most eyewitnesses are found several weeks later and pressured to come clean by the police, he fled as far as he could without a passport, to Oakland, California; and (3) instead of clamming up, he took extraordinary lengths to tell everyone but the police everything he had seen before heading cross-country.

According to Byrd's hearsay, Jake had shot both men following an argument in front of the bar. The police, before deciding to rely on the evidence they had rather than the evidence they had to work for, enlisted the Oakland police department to help them interview Byrd. Their efforts were minimal before the arrest of Fields, and, not surprisingly, nonexistent afterward. But we did not have the luxury of ignoring Mr. Byrd, and we were lucky enough to know a terrific investigator in the Bay Area, Nancy Pemberton. She set up a surveillance of his known address, and eventually came face to face with him outside his apartment building, whereupon he denied having any idea who Victor Byrd was. When she pulled out his photograph and a subpoena, he turned and ran off down the street. This was as close to thrilling as the investigation got. We persuaded a Philadelphia judge to issue a material witness warrant for Byrd, and an Oakland judge did the same; but ultimately our love for Mr. Byrd went unrequited, and no member of the defense team ever laid eyes on him again.

Rafiq was furious at our inability to persuade Byrd to testify on his behalf. He felt that our efforts had been less than stellar, and that other inmates, with far better attorneys than us, had managed to find witnesses more recalcitrant than Byrd. There are homicides getting thrown out left and right back there, he said, jerking his arm toward the cellblock. Who, I asked. This was a mistake I'd made often with Rafiq—while my partner stayed calm and nodded his head sagely, I questioned. You don't know because you don't want to know, Rafiq said. I said I was disappointed that Byrd had eluded us; then I moved on to a sticking point between us that had been left unspoken— Byrd, while claiming that Jake had been the shooter, nonetheless mentioned Smokes along with several others who had been at the scene of the crime. One thing's for sure and two things for certain, Rafiq replied. No one is right all the time.

The Client

Capital defense teams are archaeologists. It is our job to dig up every single detail about our client's past, and then reorganize those details so that a jury might feel it has received a reasonable explanation for a terrible act. So before too long we knew quite a bit about Rafiq Fields. Stories abound of the humanity that lies just beneath the surface of our most violent citizens—indeed I have known many inmates for whom it is impossible to imagine the behavior attributed to them. Rafiq Fields, however, was not one of them. He was disagreeable and argumentative from the start, and he played one team member against the other with the skill of a *Survivor* contestant trying to stay on the island. Nothing could satisfy him, and no matter how many motions we filed or witnesses we tracked down or holiday visits we made to see him, his concerns that we were against him could not be allayed. Then we found out why: Rafiq Fields had a long history of schizophrenia, and had been committed to a mental hospital a mere two weeks before the crime. A laundry list of commitments and psychological evaluations trailed behind him, and it was obvious Rafiq had suffered the lay influence of the experts whose paths he'd crossed. I have Schizo-Bifecto, he said. I, for one, wasn't going to correct him.

But mental illness is like a weed—it doesn't grow alone, and it doesn't disappear just because it's detected. Rafiq's history was replete with abuse and abandonment. He was low-functioning and drug dependent, and adamantly refused all help, including medication our own psychiatrist had prescribed. One day he would read a motion of mine and proclaim me the greatest lawyer, and best friend, he'd ever had—a few days later he would tell Dana Cook I was a disgrace to my profession. His father was long gone, and his mother was generally hostile, particularly after listening to her only son explain how we had mistreated him. And finally, there was what Rafiq called our "communication" problem: we didn't understand what he was saying, we didn't understand how his neighborhood worked, we didn't understand what kind of people the dead guys were. What he never said, through all the tantrums and silences, was that every member of our team was white, and he wasn't. Not that he was too polite to say it; rather, it was too obvious. In short, we were on one side of a chasm, and Rafiq Fields was on the other—we had no way to reach him but to keep on trying, and this we did over and over until the very day of trial.

The Investigation

After several months of interviewing witnesses from the Red Rock Lounge, we had reached two conclusions:

(1) Rafiq Fields, known to his acquaintances as Smokes, had been outside the bar at the time of the shooting. Were it not for his insistence otherwise, this fact would have been assumed rather than investigated. Every witness without exception mentioned Smokes as one of the men involved in the argument—the bartender, when pressed if he was sure it was Rafiq he saw, actually laughed and said, "Why, did he tell you he wasn't even there?"—but as the evidence piled up Rafiq seemed to get more enraged by it. There must be ten guys named Smokes in that area, he said. Besides, the victim said the killer was Smoke, not Smokes; it's not the same. Indeed, as we pushed further into our probe, the missing "s" played an ever-increasing role in Rafiq's theory of the crime.

(2) The victims of the shooting were men of ill repute. Both had been arrested numerous times for violent offenses, and even the commonwealth's witnesses had one of the victims waving a gun around in a threatening manner. The same bartender who laughed at the idea that Rafiq wasn't there had

this to say about the gun-toting John Jackson: the guy looked for trouble every day of his life; no one could pick a fight with a complete stranger as easily as he could. In short, the case set up like a perfect self-defense—violent victims, threatening behavior, a gun, and a dying declaration that Smoke did it. But when I suggested the idea, providing case law, a jury instruction, and my explanation that self-defense was real and legal, Rafiq stood up in a huff and walked out of the interview booth. "He just doesn't get it," he said, clearly to himself.

The investigation continued. Our next three targets were in some form of custody, which made things easier. First we went to Arnold Newcombe, who was on house arrest for a drug and gun charge just around the corner from the Red Rock Lounge. We found him on a bench outside the courtroom where he waited for his own case to be called. He confirmed that Jake had been in the bar at the time of the shooting, and admitted that he had covered for Jake by leading the police to another man named Jake. He would not say why Jake needed to be covered for, nor would he back off his identification of Smokes as the shooter; nonetheless the case was starting to smell, and Jake began to take form as a more realistic perpetrator. We moved on to Rashon Howell.

Rashon Howell was very small—he looked the part of a hoodlum who might slip barely noticed from one petty crime to the next. And had he stayed in Philadelphia he might have gone unnoticed entirely—he had walked away from his car theft arrest when the owner of the car failed to show up in court. But he instead ventured to Williamsport, home of the Little League World Series and, coincidentally, the locus of an unusual number of drug rehabilitation centers. It was this highly concentrated population of drug abusers that drew a small-time drug dealer like Howell, and the vigilant Williamsport police department that incarcerated him in the county jail.

He needed some encouragement to talk, and was extremely cautious when he did. He told us there was no doubt Smokes punched John Jackson after he was shot, then took his gun and walked up the street with it, but he may have exaggerated a bit when he told the police Smokes shot the men. Arnold Newcombe told him that Jake did the shooting by pulling out his own gun and reaching around Smokes; and then told him to say it was Smokes instead. Did he see Jake do the shooting, we asked. Rashon wouldn't say—we had to understand that Jake was not the sort of man you incriminated in any way. But if we looked to Jake as the doer, would we be right? Imperceptibly, he nodded. A fleeting vision of Victor Byrd running down the street chased by our investigator crossed my mind. So, I said, let's just get this down on paper and we'll be out of your hair. But Rashon Howell was nobody's fool—he was no more likely to put ink to paper than he was to win the lottery. No hard feelings, but what he had said was informational only.

Next was Jake. Jake Powers, who had been out celebrating his birthday. Who had engendered fear in Rashon Howell and loyalty in Arnold Newcombe and flight in Victor Byrd. We found him in a suburban jail doing county time for an inconsequential forgery. He spoke to us like a man who had nothing to hide and nothing to fear. Yes, he had been a big shot in that neighborhood, but not in years; in fact, Arnold Newcombe used to work for him. What did he mean by big shot, and what did Arnold do for him? He preferred not to say, but surely we knew how people became big shots in that neighborhood, and surely we knew that a man like him would need men like Arnold Newcombe, because you couldn't expect him to be involved in day-to-day activities. Why would people say he did this shooting? That was just talk, Jake said. No one had actually *said* he did it. And no one would. Except he didn't say that last sentence, because he didn't have to.

We had no choice but to go back to Rashon. For fifteen minutes we talked at him. This could be you instead of Rafiq, I said. How would you feel if he did what you're doing, Schwartz said. You're saving a man's life, I said. We'll make sure you're protected, Schwartz said. It would be a good thing for you to do, Dana Cook said. She had been silent until then. It's a good thing you brought her, Rashon said. And then he signed. As we were leaving, I turned back and said, "So why did Lyle Tyson say Smoke shot him?" He was confused, Rashon said. But I couldn't tell from his inflection if it was an answer, or a question.

The Meeting

We were ready to speak to the prosecutor. We had two distinct arguments to make, both of which addressed the capital nature of the crime. First, our client was very far from the worst of the worst—aside from his tortured background, the fact that he had been involuntarily committed only days before the crime made it clear he wasn't in his right mind. And while we recognized that with a dying declaration pointing to our client the commonwealth might feel duty bound to proceed to trial, the facts raised enough questions to make the case non-capital. The violence and provocation of the victims, the huge shadow over Jake Powers, the inability of either side to track down Victor Byrd, the recantation of Rashon Howell, these facts and many more suggested that a lingering doubt would always remain about guilt.

The hearsay facts, the prosecutor said.

Which are given a lot more weight when you consider the distance Byrd has put between himself and a courtroom.

You know we don't put much stock in recantations, the prosecutor said.

Yes, we knew that. This wasn't just any recantation, however; it happened to fit many of the facts of the case.

But remember that Jackson had a broken bone in his face. That's exactly what Howell said, that your guy punched him after shooting him.

And only at that moment, after the hundreds of hours I had spent on the Rafiq Fields case, did it occur to me what had been wrong with it all along. I quickly added the experience in the room. Between us, I said, there are seventy-five years of trying homicides. Has any of us ever seen a case where somebody shoots somebody else *and then* punches him? The room went silent. And in that silence the case finally came to me: two hotheads outside a bar, causing trouble, waving a gun, threatening Smokes. Jake coming out of the bar angry, because this is his neighborhood and who are these loudmouths disrespecting his birthday? And after he reaches around Smokes and shoots them, there's Smokes, fuming from alcohol and mental illness and maybe just who he is. So he bends down and punches Jackson in the face, then takes the gun he was threatened with and walks off with it. Of course.

The prosecutor said he would get back to us. As we were gathering our things, he tapped me on the elbow. So why did Tyson say Smoke shot him, he asked. He was confused, I said.

The Investigation

But how does a guy get that confused? The whole presumption of a dying declaration is that no one would lie if they thought they were actually dying; and besides, the evidence provided no motive for him to lie. Was it really possible that he did not see Jake reach around our client and shoot him? Something still was missing.

Days went by. We pored through the police paperwork,

reexamined every statement, revisited the crime scene, which by now had changed its name for the third time. The men had spent several hours there that night, and John Jackson was very drunk according to the toxicology report prepared by the medical examiner. But Tyson, who had made it around the corner, was only barely over the limit according to the same examiner. And that's when it occurred to us that he had not gotten to the morgue until hours after Jackson; the police had taken him to the hospital instead. Sure enough, medical personnel had drawn blood before he passed. A quick call to the hospital told us what we had missed—Tyson's alcohol level was almost four times the legal limit. He had, in fact, been confused.

Five days later the prosecutor walked into a common pleas courtroom in Philadelphia and dismissed all charges.

Aftermath

I was certain that Rafiq Fields would come into my office on his first day of freedom, give each of the team members a hug, and then spend a pleasant hour or so allowing us to bask in his hard-won freedom. I don't know why I thought this—nothing we had done had remedied his deep-seated mental illness, his fundamental distrust of authority, or his bitterness at being kept in prison for a crime he had not committed. And in fact he did not show up that first day, or ever. But four months later I received a call from a public defender in Delaware County that Rafiq had been arrested, and was tangentially involved in a drug deal. He called me for bail purposes, because the double murder, although dismissed, still loomed large in the judge's eyes. I explained the circumstances of the murder charge, and several weeks later Rafiq made bail. I never learned what happened to the drug case, because a month later Dana Cook advised me she had heard from another client that Rafiq had been murdered. To this day I have made no effort to confirm whether it is true or not. And of course you cannot confirm it either. Rafiq Fields is not my client's name—in fact no names, other than Schwartz, Cook, and Pemberton are real. The story is not to be confirmed, the truth not to be completely known. The imperfections of our criminal justice system merely amplify the imperfections of our lives. That much is for sure, that much is for certain.

Afterword

The last Beatles concert, on August 29, 1966, at Candlestick Park in San Francisco, did not sell out. No one knew it would turn out to be their last show, and 17,500 tickets went unsold. The concerts had become unpleasant—for the Beatles themselves and for a fan base who could no longer hear the music—but there was no formal announcement that they planned to stop performing live. They simply concluded that their time and effort would be better spent producing music in the studio. The decision, a long time coming for the band, only appeared sudden to a music world that assumed the Beatles would always be with us. More typically we are able to observe a decline before the disappearance sets in—the last stagecoach, the last passenger pigeon, the last soldier to die in a war that is winding down. And like a war in its last gasps—with random casualties and indiscriminate aggressions—the decline in the death penalty is observable as well. Executions and death sentences have dropped more than 75 percent from their highs of two decades ago, and there is no evidence to suggest that such trends will reverse themselves. When capital punishment ends, as it inevitably must, there will be no formal announcement or sudden decision; rather, it will grind to a slow and painful halt after an accumulation of wrongs.

The essays in this collection are not isolated instances of injustice, but rather are emblematic of the causes of this steady decline. In other words, if you write an essay about a lawyer who drank a quart of vodka a night while representing a client in a capital murder trial, you have to be prepared to face the allegation that you're selectively choosing an egregious case to make your point. The same claim might fairly apply if you told the story of a judge who created an irrevocable trust preventing distribution unless his children married white Christians of the opposite sex, and referred to "filthy Jews" in routine conversation, yet presided over a trial that sent a Jewish man to death row. And surely a defendant executed after a juror admitted he sentenced the man to death based on a rationale that involved the n-word would be the extreme exception to the right of a fair trial by an impartial jury. If these essays are indeed aberrant examples of death sentences gone awry, then the moral consequence of this collection is limited. But do they in fact represent just a few outrageous examples of an otherwise successful capital punishment system?

Kenneth Fults wouldn't have thought so. As his execution neared, another case with a racist juror had already surfaced—the Supreme Court agreed to hear the appeal of a Mexican man in Colorado judged by a juror who declared to his fellow jurors that "nine times out of ten Mexican men were guilty of being aggressive toward women and young girls." That case did not help Fults, however. His execution in Georgia was treated routinely, generating barely a ripple on social media, as if no one was surprised that a racist juror might sit in judgment. But one year after that, the Supreme Court halted the execution of another Georgia man, Keith Tharpe, when it was disclosed that a white juror in his case had stated "after studying the bible, [he] wondered if black people even have souls." At least those jurors had hidden their racism until they were in the deliberation room. In Andre Thomas's case, four jurors actually noted on their jury questionnaires that they opposed interracial marriage, prompting his lawyers to do . . . nothing. Racist jurors, sometimes enabled by prosecutors and defense attorneys, find their way onto capital juries more often than you'd like to believe.

But racism in the courtroom doesn't stop at the bar of the court. Randy Halprin's Judaism was no secret during his capital murder trial, but the judge's anti-Semitism was. His staff knew, and his family knew, and anyone aware of the irrevocable trust he had set up requiring his children to marry white Christians of the opposite sex knew. None of them came forward. But word occasionally gets out. In Pennsylvania, the child-sex investigation of Penn State assistant football coach Jerry Sandusky inadvertently led to a bigger inquiry: an email scandal the media labeled "Porngate." The salacious nickname diverted the public from a far more pernicious issue: a group of prosecutors from the Attorney General's Office had been exchanging racist and misogynistic images with judges in various courts across the state. By the time the scandal petered out, two justices on the Pennsylvania Supreme Court had been forced to resign. In the year the emails were first released, the court had heard more than two dozen capital appeals, many of them prosecuted by the Attorney General's Office. Virtually all of the cases upheld death sentences, and virtually all of those sentences still stand. The real question is not whether racist judges presiding in death penalty cases are anomalous, but rather how many are hiding their racism from public view.

And then there are the attorneys who are appointed by the court to handle our most serious criminal trials. Robert Holsey's lawyer drank a quart of vodka every night of his client's trial, but plenty of alcoholic lawyers have handled capital cases, and one even responded to a "Help Wanted" sign posted by a Kentucky judge on his courtroom door. Lawyers have slept through death penalty trials and missed crucial deadlines in capital appeals; a Georgia lawyer was parking his car during crucial testimony, and gave an eighty-seven-word closing argument in the penalty phase of his client's case. In Philadelphia, one lawyer forgot to ask his client how old he was at the time of the crime, thus allowing a juvenile to think he was going to be executed for two years before the mistake was discovered. Another argued to a jury that "an eye for an eye" only applied to the killing of a pregnant woman, somehow forgetting that his client had been convicted of that very crime. In this company, a drunken lawyer might actually be in demand.

Given such competition, it is fair to ask why prosecutors feel the need to commit misconduct in capital cases. Yet every state has a story to tell, and some have many. In the two years before the Delaware Supreme Court found its death penalty unconstitutional, three death sentences were reversed when prosecutors forgot to mention that they had dropped charges against a key witness, withheld exculpatory evidence about alternate suspects, and committed seven ethical violations in a single case. In Arizona, appellate courts found that six different "prosecutor(s) of the year" had committed prosecutorial misconduct in capital cases. In California, a secret network of jailhouse informants hidden from the defense derailed a death penalty prosecution for the largest mass killing in Orange County.

Philadelphia alone is practically a petri dish for prosecutorial misconduct. In the last year, three men were exonerated after spending years on death row. Walter Ogrod went directly from death row to freedom when he learned that the commonwealth had hidden the true cause of death as well as the severe mental health problems of a key informant. Christopher Williams was exonerated when alternative suspects turned up years later in police files and a secret deal with a co-defendant—who said that a prosecutor met with him repeatedly before the trial, coerced his testimony, and fed him fabricated information—came to light.

Then there was Kareem Johnson, whose case summed up the confluence of prosecutorial misconduct and awful defense lawyering best of all. He went to death row for nine years based on very powerful evidence: a hat found at the scene of a murder had a speck of Johnson's DNA (as well as DNA from others) on the sweatband and the blood of the victim on the brim. The commonwealth's theory was obvious enough—Johnson had been so close to the victim when he shot him that the victim's blood splashed onto the hat, which fell off Johnson's head when he fled. "This is the killer's hat," the prosecutor intoned to the jury. "Physical evidence has no bias. Physical evidence cannot lie. Physical evidence does not want to lie. Physical evidence cannot be intimidated. Physical evidence cannot be killed . . . This overwhelming physical evidence says that killer's hat was left out there on the scene." Surely this was a strong case, made even stronger by the testimony of a police officer at the scene of the crime, who testified under oath that he saw fresh drops of blood dripping off the brim of the hat. There was only one problem—there was no blood on that hat at all. Anyone looking at the DNA report might have spotted this rudimentary mistake, but apparently the defense attorneys didn't think it important enough to review the physical evidence. The prosecutor, in the words of the Pennsylvania Supreme Court, tried the case with "a reckless disregard for consequences and for the very real possibility of harm stemming from the lack of thoroughness in preparing for a first-degree murder trial." Yet even the Supreme Court failed to explain the mysterious testimony of the police officer who saw "fresh" drops of blood on a hat that actually had no blood on it at all. A judge who reviewed the evidence years after the conviction summed things up as a "gross series of almost unimaginable mistakes." Which seems to be putting it kindly.

Patterns emerge from death row. While racism plays a driving force on both sides of the aisle and from the bench, and inept defense lawyering often goes hand in hand with prosecutorial misconduct, there is another impelling cause of death sentences—severe mental illness. Andre Thomas remains on Texas's death row even after he blinded himself and ate the second eyeball. In North Carolina, Guy Tobias LeGrande represented himself at trial wearing a Superman T-shirt while claiming he was receiving messages through the television from Oprah Winfrey and Dan Rather. He called the jurors the Antichrists, which perhaps explains why they deliberated a mere fifty-three minutes before sentencing him to death. Bill Paul Marquardt remains on Florida's death row despite his paranoid schizophrenic delusions that he is the prophet of God that Nostradamus predicted, that he has been given (via voices in his head) a new version of the Biblical Book of Revelations to write, and that he can use string theory and/or quantum mechanics to save his parents (who are both deceased) and stop people from aging. Putting such people on death row instead of in secure treatment facilities is an embarrassment to our humanity.

Finally, there is the capriciousness of the capital punishment system, and what public policy operates on the basis of capriciousness? Beauford White was executed after a 12–0 vote for life by the jury. Russell Weinberger and Felix Rodriguez would still be in prison had another man not confessed years later. But for pure caprice, consider the Texas case of Michael Richard. On the day of his scheduled execution, the U.S. Supreme Court decided it would examine the lethal injection protocol to determine its constitutionality. Of course Richard's lawyers were fully aware of the development that was going to spare their client, but that day of all days they were having computer problems. When they called the courthouse to advise the court that their petition to stay Richard's execution might be a few minutes late, the presiding judge of the Texas Court of Criminal Appeals, Sharon Keller, uttered these immortal and immoral words: "We close at five." Richard was executed that night. The man scheduled to be executed in Texas two days later received a stay that Richard would have received had the courtroom doors remained open. As for Keller, the *New York Times* and two dozen ethics experts called for her removal, but fourteen years later, she is still the presiding judge of that court.

Of course, any human endeavor is going to bring with it a degree of error, but is *error* really the right word for the coercion of two confessions or the arbitrariness of who gets executed or the simple meanness of a judge who closes a door knowing a man's life depends on it being open? If not error, what is the right word? We should at least avoid labeling such events as bad luck, though luck and misfortune will inevitably seep into any discussion about capital punishment. For every drunken lawyer representing a client sentenced to death, ten are able to avoid it; and for every prosecutor who hides a police report and gets caught, a hundred get away with it. Justice Potter Stewart, in *Furman v. Georgia*, wrote that death sentences were cruel and unusual "in the same way that being struck by lightning is cruel and unusual." That was nearly fifty years ago, and very little has changed in this regard. Our capital punishment is that most unsettling of words—*arbitrary*.

Stephen Bright, the founder of the Southern Center for Human Rights, says that the criminal courts are the part of society least affected by the civil rights movement. He is right, of course; but as injustices slowly find their way into the public ether, the community becomes less enthralled with the death penalty as a solution to a justice problem. The election of progressive prosecutors makes a call for the ultimate punishment less politic. The depletion of civic coffers makes it impossible to justify the cost of capital punishment, which is three times that of a life sentence. And the Black Lives Matter movement makes it harder to overlook endemic racism. DNA results have proven our fallibility, and the opening of prosecutors' files has given us an uncomfortable view of the misconduct we are willing to engage in for a capital conviction. The results are not in the rhetoric but in the data—death sentences and executions are at their lowest levels in decades. Change is just around the corner.

By now you might have forgotten about the epigraph at the beginning of this afterword. Charles Lightoller was the senior officer to survive the *Titanic*; it fell to him to tell the story of failure that was the sinking of an unsinkable ship. His quote is oddly relevant to the world of capital punishment, a world where misconduct is spotted but not punished, where biases and racism are rotting but not revealed, where injustices are argued but not recognized. Lightoller heard reports that ice was out there, but he didn't reckon with those reports until he saw the damage that had been done. The essays in this collection illuminate the misconduct, the biases and racism, the injustices of capital punishment; it is long past time to reckon with them. That illumination is only meaningful if a more obvious point is understood—these stories are more the rule than the exception. And maybe that's the best reason to quote Charles Lightoller. He was a man who knew the tip of an iceberg when he saw it.

Acknowledgments

When you've spent your entire professional life working as a public defender or running a small organization against the death penalty, finding a progressive nonprofit willing to publish a collection of essays against the death penalty is like winning the lottery by betting on the numbers in your birthday. I will be forever grateful to The New Press for giving this collection the opportunity to reach a wider audience; and in particular I want to thank zakia henderson-brown for shaping the work, recognizing the power of the stories, and making sure the writing didn't get in the way. Perhaps most important of all, zakia reminded me that these essays reflect a trauma well beyond the stories themselves, and that my writing had to respect it.

I don't know if I would have been on The New Press's radar were it not for my good friend Steve Bright. The founder of the Southern Center for Human Rights and an icon in the anti–death penalty community, Steve introduced me to them and gave my essays what I can only describe as street cred. To paraphrase the old commercial, when Steve Bright talks, people listen.

Although I have been writing most of my life, I've never

gotten to the point where I trusted my own writing enough to send it to strangers (and yes, all editors are strangers—just ask them) before friends. For this reason I want to thank my most loyal late night and early morning readers, Maurie Levin and Richard Shore. Their willingness to tell me when something is right, or wrong, was invaluable.

Stu Schuman, my late mentor at the Defender Association of Philadelphia, insisted that I read his very rare copy of *Star Wormwood* when I was just starting out as a defender. His influence over the way I think about indigent defense and capital punishment is immeasurable.

Finally, I need to recognize those who can't be acknowledged. The publication of this collection is not an "I'd like to thank the Academy, the key grip, and my wardrobe assistant" type of occasion. But while these essays are about pain and death and injustice, there is resilience and hope in them as well. The web of capital punishment is wide but thin, and those fighting against it are close to breaking through. Each one of these stories has many protagonists working tirelessly on behalf of the person ensnared in that web, and though there are too many to name, they know who they are.

About the Author

Marc Bookman is the executive director of the Atlantic Center for Capital Representation, a nonprofit that provides services for those facing possible execution. Before that he spent many years in the Homicide Unit of the Defender Association of Philadelphia. He has published essays in *The Atlantic*, *Mother Jones*, *VICE*, and *Slate*. He lives in Philadelphia, and this is his first book.

Publishing in the Public Interest

Thank you for reading this book published by The New Press. The New Press is a nonprofit, public interest publisher. New Press books and authors play a crucial role in sparking conversations about the key political and social issues of our day.

We hope you enjoyed this book and that you will stay in touch with The New Press. Here are a few ways to stay up to date with our books, events, and the issues we cover:

- Sign up at www.thenewpress.com/subscribe to receive updates on New Press authors and issues and to be notified about local events
- Like us on Facebook: www.facebook.com/newpress books
- Follow us on Twitter: www.twitter.com/thenewpress
- Follow us on Instagram: www.instagram.com/the newpress

Please consider buying New Press books for yourself; for friends and family; or to donate to schools, libraries, community centers, prison libraries, and other organizations involved with the issues our authors write about.

The New Press is a 501(c)(3) nonprofit organization. You can also support our work with a tax-deductible gift by visiting www.thenewpress.com/donate.